50 Japan Summer Season Recipes for Home

By: Kelly Johnson

Table of Contents

- Miso Shiru (Miso Soup)
- Cold Soba Noodles
- Hiyashi Chuka (Cold Chinese Noodles)
- Ebi (Shrimp) Tempura
- Tofu Salad
- Japanese Cucumber Salad
- Okonomiyaki (Japanese Savory Pancake)
- Takoyaki (Octopus Balls)
- Yakitori (Grilled Chicken Skewers)
- Goya Champuru (Bitter Melon Stir-Fry)
- Edamame Beans
- Chawanmushi (Savory Egg Custard)
- Agedashi Tofu (Fried Tofu in Dashi)
- Udon Noodle Salad
- Yudofu (Hot Tofu Stew)
- Goya Stir-Fry
- Shiso and Lemon Rice
- Cold Soba with Dipping Sauce
- Sunomono (Vinegared Salad)
- Japanese Pickles (Tsukemono)
- Yaki Onigiri (Grilled Rice Balls)
- Seaweed Salad
- Sashimi Salad
- Salmon Teriyaki
- Miso-Marinated Grilled Eggplant
- Cold Chashu Ramen
- Mentaiko Pasta (Spicy Cod Roe Pasta)
- Japanese Corn Tempura
- Zaru Udon (Cold Udon Noodles)
- Ikayaki (Grilled Whole Squid)
- Sweet Corn Soup
- Tuna Tataki

- Japanese Style Potato Salad
- Shrimp and Avocado Salad
- Nasu Dengaku (Miso Glazed Eggplant)
- Tonkotsu Ramen (Pork Bone Broth Ramen)
- Agedashi Eggplant
- Umeboshi (Pickled Plum) Rice Balls
- Japanese Summer Rolls
- Cold Tofu with Soy Sauce and Green Onions
- Okra with Soy Sauce and Sesame
- Grilled Mackerel
- Chicken Karaage (Japanese Fried Chicken)
- Spicy Tuna Sushi Rolls
- Teriyaki Chicken Salad
- Japanese Fruit Parfait
- Soba Noodle Soup
- Yakisoba (Fried Noodles)
- Miso-Glazed Zucchini
- Summer Vegetable Tempura

Miso Shiru (Miso Soup)

Ingredients:

- **4 cups** dashi (Japanese stock, homemade or instant)
- **3-4 tablespoons** miso paste (white or red, to taste)
- **1/2 cup** tofu (cubed, firm or silken)
- **1/4 cup** sliced green onions
- **1/4 cup** wakame seaweed (dried and soaked, optional)
- **1/2 cup** mushrooms (shiitake or enoki, optional)
- **1 tablespoon** soy sauce (optional, for extra flavor)

Instructions:

1. **Prepare the Dashi:**
   - If using instant dashi, dissolve the granules in 4 cups of water according to the package instructions. If using homemade dashi, heat it up to a simmer.
2. **Add the Tofu:**
   - Cut the tofu into small cubes and gently add them to the simmering dashi. Allow them to heat through for about 2-3 minutes.
3. **Prepare Miso Paste:**
   - In a small bowl, ladle out a small amount of hot dashi and whisk it with the miso paste until smooth. This helps to dissolve the miso paste more easily.
4. **Add Miso to the Soup:**
   - Stir the miso mixture back into the pot with the dashi. Do not let the soup boil after adding the miso, as this can alter its flavor and texture.
5. **Add Additional Ingredients:**
   - If using wakame seaweed, mushrooms, or additional vegetables, add them at this stage and simmer for a few minutes until they are tender.
6. **Season the Soup:**
   - Taste the soup and adjust the seasoning with soy sauce if needed.
7. **Serve:**
   - Ladle the soup into bowls and garnish with sliced green onions.

Tips:

- **Wakame Seaweed:** Soak dried wakame in water for a few minutes before adding it to the soup. It will rehydrate and expand.
- **Miso Type:** White miso is milder and sweeter, while red miso is stronger and saltier. Adjust according to your preference.
- **Vegetables:** Feel free to add other seasonal vegetables or proteins as desired.

Enjoy your homemade Miso Shiru!

Cold Soba Noodles

Ingredients:

- **8 ounces** soba noodles
- **2 cups** dashi (or substitute with vegetable broth)
- **1/4 cup** soy sauce
- **1/4 cup** mirin
- **1 tablespoon** sugar
- **1 teaspoon** sesame oil
- **2-3 green onions** (thinly sliced)
- **1/2 cup** cucumber (julienned)
- **1/2 cup** shredded nori (seaweed)
- **1 tablespoon** sesame seeds (toasted)
- **Pickled ginger** (optional, for garnish)
- **Wasabi** (optional, for garnish)

Instructions:

1. **Cook the Soba Noodles:**
   - Bring a large pot of water to a boil. Add the soba noodles and cook according to the package instructions (usually about 4-5 minutes). Stir occasionally to prevent sticking.
   - Once cooked, drain the noodles and rinse them under cold running water to cool them down and remove excess starch. Drain well and set aside.
2. **Prepare the Dipping Sauce:**
   - In a bowl, mix together the dashi, soy sauce, mirin, sugar, and sesame oil. Stir until the sugar is dissolved. Adjust the seasoning to taste if needed. Chill in the refrigerator until ready to serve.
3. **Assemble the Noodles:**
   - Divide the cold soba noodles into serving bowls or plates.
4. **Garnish:**
   - Top the noodles with julienned cucumber, sliced green onions, shredded nori, and toasted sesame seeds. Add pickled ginger and wasabi on the side if desired.
5. **Serve:**
   - Serve the cold soba noodles with the chilled dipping sauce on the side. To eat, dip the noodles into the sauce and enjoy!

Tips:

- **Noodle Texture:** For a firmer texture, do not overcook the soba noodles. They should be tender but not mushy.
- **Dipping Sauce:** You can make the dipping sauce ahead of time and keep it refrigerated. Adjust the soy sauce and mirin quantities according to your taste preferences.

- **Additions:** Feel free to add other toppings such as thinly sliced radishes, grated daikon, or cooked shrimp for extra flavor and texture.

Enjoy your Cold Soba Noodles!

Hiyashi Chuka (Cold Chinese Noodles)

Ingredients:

- **8 ounces** Chinese egg noodles or other thin noodles
- **1/2 cup** cooked chicken breast or thigh, shredded (optional)
- **1/2 cup** cooked shrimp, peeled and deveined (optional)
- **1/4 cup** julienned cucumber
- **1/4 cup** julienned carrots
- **1/4 cup** thinly sliced ham or crab stick
- **1/4 cup** bean sprouts (blanched)
- **2 tablespoons** chopped fresh cilantro (optional)
- **2 tablespoons** sesame seeds (toasted)
- **2-3 radishes**, thinly sliced (optional)
- **1/4 cup** sliced green onions (for garnish)

For the Dressing:

- **3 tablespoons** soy sauce
- **3 tablespoons** rice vinegar
- **2 tablespoons** sugar
- **1 tablespoon** sesame oil
- **1 tablespoon** mirin
- **1 teaspoon** grated ginger (optional)
- **1 teaspoon** sesame seeds (toasted)
- **1 clove** garlic, minced (optional)

Instructions:

1. **Cook the Noodles:**
   - Bring a large pot of water to a boil. Cook the noodles according to the package instructions (usually about 3-4 minutes). Stir occasionally to prevent sticking.
   - Drain the noodles and rinse them under cold running water to cool them down. Drain well and set aside.
2. **Prepare the Dressing:**
   - In a bowl, whisk together soy sauce, rice vinegar, sugar, sesame oil, mirin, grated ginger, minced garlic (if using), and toasted sesame seeds until the sugar is dissolved. Adjust the seasoning to taste and chill the dressing in the refrigerator.
3. **Prepare the Toppings:**
   - While the noodles are cooling, prepare the toppings. Julienne the cucumber and carrots, slice the ham or crab sticks, and blanch the bean sprouts if needed.
4. **Assemble the Dish:**
   - Divide the cooled noodles into serving bowls or plates.
   - Arrange the toppings (cucumber, carrots, ham or crab sticks, bean sprouts, chicken, and shrimp) on top of the noodles.

5. **Serve:**
   - Drizzle the chilled dressing over the noodles and toppings. Garnish with chopped cilantro (if using), sliced radishes, and toasted sesame seeds.
   - Serve immediately, or refrigerate until ready to serve.

Tips:

- **Noodle Choice:** Use thin Chinese egg noodles or other types of thin, quick-cooking noodles.
- **Protein Options:** You can substitute or add other proteins like tofu or cooked pork if desired.
- **Vegetables:** Feel free to add or swap out vegetables based on your preferences or seasonal availability.

Enjoy your refreshing Hiyashi Chuka!

Ebi (Shrimp) Tempura

Ingredients:

- **12 large shrimp**, peeled and deveined, tails left on
- **1 cup** all-purpose flour
- **1/2 cup** cornstarch
- **1 teaspoon** baking powder
- **1 cup** ice-cold water
- **1 large egg**
- **1/2 teaspoon** salt
- **Vegetable oil** (for frying, enough to fill your pot or pan)

For Serving:

- **Tempura dipping sauce** (Tentsuyu) or soy sauce
- **Grated daikon radish** (optional, for garnish)
- **Lemon wedges** (optional, for garnish)

Instructions:

1. **Prepare the Shrimp:**
   - If not already done, peel and devein the shrimp, leaving the tails on. Pat them dry with paper towels to remove excess moisture.
2. **Prepare the Tempura Batter:**
   - In a large bowl, whisk together the flour, cornstarch, baking powder, and salt.
   - In a separate bowl, lightly beat the egg and then add the ice-cold water. Stir to combine.
   - Pour the egg mixture into the dry ingredients and stir gently. The batter should be lumpy; do not overmix. The ice-cold water helps create a light, crispy texture.
3. **Heat the Oil:**
   - Pour vegetable oil into a deep pot or fryer to a depth of about 2 inches. Heat the oil to 350°F (175°C). You can test if the oil is ready by dropping a small amount of batter into it; it should float and sizzle immediately.
4. **Coat the Shrimp:**
   - Lightly coat each shrimp with a bit of flour (this helps the batter stick better).
   - Dip each shrimp into the tempura batter, allowing excess batter to drip off.
5. **Fry the Shrimp:**
   - Carefully slide the battered shrimp into the hot oil, a few at a time to avoid overcrowding.
   - Fry until golden brown and crispy, about 2-3 minutes per side.
   - Remove the shrimp with a slotted spoon and drain on a paper towel-lined plate.
6. **Serve:**
   - Serve the hot Ebi Tempura with tempura dipping sauce (Tentsuyu) or soy sauce. Garnish with grated daikon radish and lemon wedges if desired.

Tips:

- **Batter Consistency:** Keep the batter cold and slightly lumpy for the crispiest texture. Overmixing the batter can make it dense.
- **Oil Temperature:** Maintain the oil temperature to ensure the tempura stays crispy and doesn't become greasy. Use a thermometer for accuracy.
- **Garnishes:** Serve with dipping sauces and garnishes for added flavor and presentation.

Enjoy your crispy and delicious Ebi Tempura!

Tofu Salad

Ingredients:

- **1 block (14 oz)** firm tofu
- **2 cups** mixed salad greens (such as lettuce, spinach, and arugula)
- **1/2 cup** cherry tomatoes (halved)
- **1/2 cucumber** (sliced)
- **1/4 red onion** (thinly sliced)
- **1/4 cup** shredded carrots
- **1/4 cup** radishes (thinly sliced, optional)
- **1/4 cup** avocado (cubed, optional)
- **2 tablespoons** sesame seeds (toasted, optional)
- **2-3 tablespoons** chopped fresh cilantro or parsley (optional)

For the Dressing:

- **2 tablespoons** soy sauce
- **1 tablespoon** rice vinegar
- **1 tablespoon** sesame oil
- **1 teaspoon** honey or maple syrup (optional, for a touch of sweetness)
- **1 teaspoon** grated ginger
- **1 clove** garlic, minced
- **1 teaspoon** toasted sesame seeds (optional, for extra flavor)

Instructions:

1. **Prepare the Tofu:**
   - Drain the tofu and press it to remove excess moisture. You can use a tofu press or wrap it in paper towels and place a weight on top.
   - Cut the tofu into bite-sized cubes.
   - Heat a non-stick skillet over medium-high heat and add a small amount of oil. Add the tofu cubes and cook, turning occasionally, until golden and crispy on all sides, about 8-10 minutes. Remove from heat and let cool.
2. **Prepare the Vegetables:**
   - While the tofu is cooling, prepare the salad ingredients: wash and chop the greens, halve the cherry tomatoes, slice the cucumber and radishes, and shred the carrots. Cube the avocado if using.
3. **Make the Dressing:**
   - In a small bowl, whisk together soy sauce, rice vinegar, sesame oil, honey or maple syrup (if using), grated ginger, minced garlic, and toasted sesame seeds.
4. **Assemble the Salad:**
   - In a large bowl, combine the mixed greens, cherry tomatoes, cucumber, red onion, shredded carrots, and radishes.
   - Add the cooled tofu cubes on top.

- Drizzle the dressing over the salad and toss gently to coat all ingredients.
5. **Garnish and Serve:**
    - Garnish with avocado cubes, toasted sesame seeds, and chopped fresh cilantro or parsley if desired.
    - Serve immediately for the freshest taste, or chill in the refrigerator until ready to serve.

Tips:

- **Tofu Texture:** For extra crispy tofu, use extra-firm tofu and ensure it's well-drained and pressed.
- **Customization:** Feel free to add other vegetables, nuts, or seeds according to your preference.
- **Dressing Variations:** Adjust the dressing ingredients to suit your taste, adding more honey for sweetness or more soy sauce for saltiness.

Enjoy your vibrant and tasty Tofu Salad!

Japanese Cucumber Salad

Ingredients:

- **2 medium cucumbers** (preferably Japanese or English cucumbers)
- **1/2 teaspoon** salt
- **2 tablespoons** rice vinegar
- **1 tablespoon** soy sauce
- **1 tablespoon** sugar
- **1 teaspoon** sesame oil
- **1 teaspoon** sesame seeds (toasted)
- **1 tablespoon** thinly sliced nori (seaweed) (optional)
- **1 tablespoon** pickled ginger (optional, for garnish)
- **1/4 cup** thinly sliced radishes (optional, for added crunch and color)

Instructions:

1. **Prepare the Cucumbers:**
   - Wash and slice the cucumbers thinly, ideally using a mandoline slicer for uniform thickness.
   - Place the cucumber slices in a colander and sprinkle with salt. Let them sit for about 10 minutes to allow the salt to draw out excess moisture.
2. **Rinse and Dry:**
   - Rinse the cucumbers thoroughly under cold running water to remove excess salt.
   - Pat the cucumber slices dry with paper towels or a clean kitchen cloth.
3. **Prepare the Dressing:**
   - In a small bowl, whisk together rice vinegar, soy sauce, sugar, and sesame oil until the sugar is dissolved.
4. **Assemble the Salad:**
   - Place the dried cucumber slices in a large bowl.
   - Pour the dressing over the cucumbers and toss gently to coat evenly.
5. **Garnish and Serve:**
   - Sprinkle toasted sesame seeds and thinly sliced nori over the top.
   - Garnish with pickled ginger and radishes if using.
   - Serve immediately or chill in the refrigerator for about 15-20 minutes to let the flavors meld.

Tips:

- **Cucumber Type:** Japanese or English cucumbers are ideal because they have fewer seeds and a thinner skin. If using regular cucumbers, you may want to peel them and remove the seeds.
- **Texture:** For extra crunch, you can slice the cucumbers into thin rounds or julienne them.

- **Adjusting Flavor:** Adjust the amount of sugar or soy sauce based on your taste preferences. You can also add a little bit of grated ginger for an extra kick.

Enjoy this crisp and tangy Japanese Cucumber Salad!

Okonomiyaki (Japanese Savory Pancake)

Ingredients:

- **2 cups** all-purpose flour
- **1 1/2 cups** dashi stock (or water if preferred)
- **2 large eggs**
- **2 cups** finely shredded cabbage
- **1/2 cup** thinly sliced green onions
- **1/2 cup** cooked bacon or pork belly, chopped (or other protein like shrimp or chicken, optional)
- **1/4 cup** pickled ginger (beni shoga), finely chopped (optional)
- **1/2 cup** grated yam or yam flour (optional, for extra fluffiness)

For the Toppings:

- **Okonomiyaki sauce** (or substitute with a mix of Worcestershire sauce and ketchup)
- **Japanese mayonnaise**
- **Aonori** (dried seaweed flakes, optional)
- **Katsuobushi** (dried bonito flakes, optional)
- **Extra green onions**, sliced (for garnish)
- **Sesame seeds** (optional, for garnish)

Instructions:

1. **Prepare the Batter:**
   - In a large bowl, whisk together the flour and dashi stock (or water) until smooth.
   - Add the eggs and mix well.
   - Fold in the shredded cabbage, green onions, pickled ginger, and grated yam or yam flour (if using). Mix until all ingredients are well combined.
2. **Cook the Okonomiyaki:**
   - Heat a non-stick skillet or griddle over medium heat and lightly grease with oil.
   - Pour about 1/2 cup of the batter onto the skillet and spread it into a round shape, about 1/2 inch thick.
   - Add a portion of the chopped bacon or pork belly on top of the batter.
   - Cook for about 3-4 minutes until the bottom is golden brown and crispy. Flip carefully and cook the other side for another 3-4 minutes until cooked through and golden brown.
3. **Add Toppings:**
   - Once cooked, transfer the Okonomiyaki to a serving plate.
   - Drizzle with Okonomiyaki sauce and Japanese mayonnaise.
   - Sprinkle with aonori and katsuobushi if desired.
   - Garnish with extra green onions and sesame seeds if you like.
4. **Serve:**
   - Serve hot, cut into wedges, and enjoy!

Tips:

- **Batter Consistency:** The batter should be thick but pourable. If it's too thick, add a little more dashi or water; if too thin, add a bit more flour.
- **Ingredients:** Feel free to customize the fillings based on your preference. Popular additions include mushrooms, corn, or even cheese.
- **Flipping:** Use a large spatula to help flip the Okonomiyaki to avoid breaking it. If you're making larger Okonomiyaki, you might need to cook them in batches.

Enjoy making and eating this savory, customizable Japanese pancake!

Takoyaki (Octopus Balls)

Ingredients:

- **1 cup** all-purpose flour
- **1 1/2 cups** dashi stock (or water)
- **2 large eggs**
- **1/2 cup** cooked octopus (chopped into small pieces)
- **1/4 cup** chopped green onions
- **1/4 cup** tenkasu (tempura scraps) (optional)
- **1/4 cup** pickled ginger (beni shoga), finely chopped
- **1/4 cup** chopped fresh parsley (optional)

For the Takoyaki Sauce:

- **1/4 cup** okonomiyaki sauce (or substitute with a mix of Worcestershire sauce and ketchup)
- **2 tablespoons** soy sauce

For Garnish:

- **Takoyaki sauce** (store-bought or homemade)
- **Japanese mayonnaise**
- **Aonori** (dried seaweed flakes)
- **Katsuobushi** (dried bonito flakes)
- **Extra chopped green onions** (optional)

Equipment:

- **Takoyaki pan** (available at Asian markets or online)
- **Takoyaki picks or skewers**

Instructions:

1. **Prepare the Batter:**
   - In a large bowl, whisk together the flour and dashi stock until smooth.
   - Add the eggs and mix until well combined.
2. **Preheat the Takoyaki Pan:**
   - Place the takoyaki pan over medium heat. Lightly brush each hole with vegetable oil to prevent sticking.
3. **Cook the Takoyaki:**
   - Pour the batter into each hole of the pan, filling each well almost to the top.
   - Add a small piece of chopped octopus to each hole.
   - Sprinkle green onions, tenkasu, pickled ginger, and parsley (if using) over the batter.
   - Let the batter cook for about 1-2 minutes until the edges start to set.

4. **Turn the Takoyaki Balls:**
   - Using takoyaki picks or skewers, start turning the balls by inserting the pick into the edges of the batter and rotating it to form a ball shape. This requires some practice to get a uniform shape and ensure even cooking.
   - Continue cooking and turning the takoyaki until they are golden brown and crispy on the outside, about 3-4 more minutes.
5. **Prepare the Takoyaki Sauce:**
   - In a small bowl, mix together the okonomiyaki sauce and soy sauce.
6. **Serve:**
   - Remove the cooked takoyaki balls from the pan and transfer them to a serving plate.
   - Drizzle with takoyaki sauce and Japanese mayonnaise.
   - Sprinkle with aonori and katsuobushi.
   - Garnish with extra green onions if desired.

Tips:

- **Batter Consistency:** The batter should be slightly thin so it can easily flow into the takoyaki holes. Adjust with additional dashi or flour if necessary.
- **Octopus:** Pre-cooked octopus can be found at Asian grocery stores, or you can boil it yourself. Make sure it's finely chopped.
- **Pan:** If you don't have a takoyaki pan, you can try using a regular muffin tin, though the shape and texture might differ.

Enjoy your homemade Takoyaki, a fun and tasty treat perfect for gatherings or a special snack!

Yakitori (Grilled Chicken Skewers)

Ingredients:

- **1 pound** chicken thighs (boneless, skinless), cut into bite-sized pieces
- **1-2 tablespoons** vegetable oil (for grilling)

For the Yakitori Sauce (Tare):

- **1/2 cup** soy sauce
- **1/4 cup** mirin
- **1/4 cup** sake
- **2 tablespoons** sugar
- **1 tablespoon** rice vinegar (optional, for a bit of acidity)

Optional Garnishes:

- **1 tablespoon** sesame seeds (toasted)
- **2-3 green onions**, sliced
- **Shichimi togarashi** (Japanese chili pepper mix, optional)

Instructions:

1. **Prepare the Yakitori Sauce (Tare):**
   - In a small saucepan, combine soy sauce, mirin, sake, and sugar.
   - Bring to a simmer over medium heat, stirring occasionally until the sugar dissolves and the sauce thickens slightly, about 5-10 minutes.
   - Remove from heat and let it cool. If using rice vinegar, stir it in after removing from heat. Set aside.
2. **Prepare the Chicken:**
   - Cut the chicken thighs into bite-sized pieces. If you prefer, you can also use other parts of the chicken, such as chicken breast or tenders.
   - Thread the chicken pieces onto skewers, leaving a bit of space between each piece. If using wooden skewers, soak them in water for 30 minutes before grilling to prevent burning.
3. **Preheat the Grill:**
   - Preheat your grill or grill pan over medium-high heat. If using a charcoal grill, let the coals get hot and ashy.
4. **Grill the Chicken:**
   - Brush the grill grates or grill pan with vegetable oil to prevent sticking.
   - Place the skewers on the grill and cook for about 2-3 minutes per side, turning occasionally, until the chicken is cooked through and has nice grill marks. You can brush the skewers with some of the yakitori sauce during the last few minutes of grilling for extra flavor.
5. **Serve:**

- Remove the skewers from the grill and brush with additional yakitori sauce if desired.
- Sprinkle with toasted sesame seeds and sliced green onions.
- Garnish with shichimi togarashi for a bit of spice if you like.

Tips:

- **Chicken Pieces:** Make sure the chicken pieces are of even size for uniform cooking.
- **Sauce Reduction:** If the sauce thickens too much after cooling, you can reheat and add a little water to thin it out.
- **Grilling:** If you prefer to use a broiler, preheat it and place the skewers under the broiler, turning them occasionally until cooked through.

Enjoy your homemade Yakitori, perfect for a casual meal or a fun party appetizer!

Goya Champuru (Bitter Melon Stir-Fry)

Ingredients:

- **1 medium bitter melon (goya)**
- **1 block (14 oz)** firm tofu
- **4 ounces** pork belly or pork shoulder (sliced thinly)
- **1 tablespoon** vegetable oil (for cooking)
- **1 small onion** (sliced thinly)
- **2 cloves garlic** (minced)
- **1 tablespoon** soy sauce
- **1 tablespoon** mirin
- **1 tablespoon** sake (or substitute with white wine)
- **1 teaspoon** sesame oil
- **1/4 teaspoon** salt (or to taste)
- **1/4 teaspoon** black pepper (or to taste)
- **2 eggs** (beaten, optional)
- **1 tablespoon** chopped fresh cilantro or green onions (for garnish)

Instructions:

1. **Prepare the Bitter Melon:**
   - Cut the bitter melon in half lengthwise and scoop out the seeds using a spoon.
   - Slice the melon thinly.
   - To reduce bitterness, sprinkle the sliced bitter melon with a bit of salt and let it sit for 10-15 minutes. Rinse thoroughly and pat dry with paper towels.
2. **Prepare the Tofu:**
   - Drain the tofu and press it to remove excess moisture. Cut it into bite-sized cubes.
   - Heat a non-stick skillet over medium heat and add a little oil. Fry the tofu cubes until golden brown on all sides. Remove from the skillet and set aside.
3. **Cook the Pork:**
   - In the same skillet, add a bit more oil if needed. Cook the sliced pork until browned and cooked through. Remove from the skillet and set aside.
4. **Stir-Fry the Vegetables:**
   - Add a bit more oil to the skillet if needed. Stir-fry the sliced onion and garlic until they are softened and fragrant.
5. **Combine Ingredients:**
   - Add the sliced bitter melon to the skillet and cook for about 3-5 minutes, stirring occasionally, until it starts to soften.
   - Return the cooked pork and tofu to the skillet. Stir to combine all the ingredients.
6. **Season and Finish:**
   - Add the soy sauce, mirin, sake, sesame oil, salt, and pepper. Stir well and cook for an additional 2-3 minutes to let the flavors meld.

- If using eggs, push the mixture to one side of the skillet and pour the beaten eggs into the empty side. Scramble the eggs until cooked through, then mix them into the rest of the dish.

7. **Serve:**
   - Garnish with chopped cilantro or green onions if desired.
   - Serve hot with steamed rice.

Tips:

- **Bitter Melon:** If you prefer less bitterness, make sure to rinse the bitter melon well after salting it.
- **Protein Options:** You can substitute the pork with chicken or beef if you prefer. Tofu can also be omitted for a vegetarian version.
- **Eggs:** Adding eggs is optional but adds richness and texture to the dish.

Enjoy your Goya Champuru—a flavorful and nutritious stir-fry with a distinctive taste!

Edamame Beans

Ingredients:

- **1 pound** frozen edamame beans (in the pod)
- **Water** (for boiling)
- **Salt** (to taste)

Optional Seasonings:

- **1 tablespoon** soy sauce
- **1 tablespoon** sesame oil
- **1/2 teaspoon** garlic powder
- **1/2 teaspoon** crushed red pepper flakes (for a bit of heat)
- **1 tablespoon** sesame seeds (toasted)
- **1 tablespoon** chopped fresh cilantro or green onions (for garnish)
- **Lemon zest** or **lemon juice** (for a fresh touch)

Instructions:

1. **Boil the Edamame:**
   - Bring a large pot of water to a boil. Add a generous amount of salt to the water.
   - Add the frozen edamame beans to the boiling water.
   - Cook for about 4-5 minutes until the edamame are tender and bright green. If using fresh edamame, they may need slightly less time.
2. **Drain and Season:**
   - Drain the edamame beans in a colander and rinse with cold water to stop the cooking process.
   - While still warm, toss the edamame with additional salt to taste.
3. **Optional Seasoning:**
   - For extra flavor, you can toss the cooked edamame with soy sauce and sesame oil, then sprinkle with garlic powder, crushed red pepper flakes, and toasted sesame seeds.
   - Garnish with chopped cilantro or green onions if desired.
   - For a fresh twist, add a bit of lemon zest or a squeeze of lemon juice before serving.
4. **Serve:**
   - Serve the edamame warm or at room temperature.

Tips:

- **Seasoning Variations:** Experiment with different seasonings based on your taste. You can use other spices like smoked paprika, curry powder, or even a touch of honey for sweetness.
- **Serving:** Edamame can be served as an appetizer, snack, or side dish. They are also great as a topping for salads or grain bowls.

Enjoy your edamame beans as a healthy and versatile snack!

Chawanmushi (Savory Egg Custard)

Ingredients:

- **3 large eggs**
- **1 1/2 cups** dashi stock (or chicken/vegetable broth)
- **1 tablespoon** soy sauce
- **1 tablespoon** mirin
- **1/2 teaspoon** salt (or to taste)
- **1/4 teaspoon** white pepper (or to taste)

Optional Fillings:

- **4-6 small shrimp**, peeled and deveined
- **2-3 mushrooms**, sliced (shiitake or enoki are great choices)
- **1/4 cup** cooked chicken, diced (or other protein like tofu)
- **1/4 cup** sliced ginkgo nuts or bamboo shoots
- **1-2 tablespoons** chopped green onions
- **1-2 tablespoons** cooked and seasoned spinach or other vegetables

Instructions:

1. **Prepare the Egg Mixture:**
   - In a bowl, gently beat the eggs until well combined. Avoid creating too many bubbles.
   - In a separate bowl, combine the dashi stock, soy sauce, mirin, salt, and white pepper. Stir to mix well.
   - Gradually add the dashi mixture to the beaten eggs, stirring gently. Strain the mixture through a fine-mesh sieve into another bowl to remove any lumps and bubbles.
2. **Prepare the Fillings:**
   - If using shrimp, mushrooms, chicken, or other fillings, lightly steam or cook them beforehand. For shrimp and chicken, briefly blanch or cook them until just done.
   - Place a small amount of each filling in the bottom of individual heatproof cups or ramekins.
3. **Pour and Steam:**
   - Carefully pour the egg mixture over the fillings in the cups. Leave a little space at the top of each cup.
   - Cover each cup with aluminum foil or a small lid to prevent water from dripping into the custard.
   - Steam the cups over a pot of simmering water (not boiling) for about 15-20 minutes, or until the custard is set. You can check by inserting a skewer or toothpick into the center; it should come out clean when done.
4. **Serve:**
   - Once the chawanmushi is cooked, carefully remove the cups from the steamer.

- Garnish with extra green onions or a drizzle of soy sauce if desired.
- Serve hot or warm.

Tips:

- **Steaming:** The key to a smooth chawanmushi is to steam it gently and avoid high heat. Boiling water can create bubbles and disrupt the custard texture.
- **Custard Texture:** Ensure that the egg mixture is well-strained to achieve a silky texture. Stir gently to avoid bubbles.
- **Fillings:** Customize the fillings based on your preferences. Common variations include adding small pieces of cooked fish, crab, or other vegetables.

Enjoy this elegant and comforting Japanese dish!

Agedashi Tofu (Fried Tofu in Dashi)

Ingredients:

- **1 block (14 oz)** firm tofu
- **1/4 cup** all-purpose flour
- **1/4 cup** cornstarch
- **Vegetable oil** (for frying, enough to fill your pan to about 1/2 inch depth)

For the Dashi Sauce:

- **1 cup** dashi stock (or chicken/vegetable broth)
- **2 tablespoons** soy sauce
- **2 tablespoons** mirin
- **1 tablespoon** sake (or substitute with white wine)
- **1 teaspoon** sugar (optional, for a touch of sweetness)

Garnishes:

- **Grated daikon radish** (optional)
- **Chopped green onions**
- **Shredded nori** (dried seaweed)
- **Grated ginger** (optional)

Instructions:

1. **Prepare the Tofu:**
   - Drain the tofu and press it to remove excess moisture. You can use a tofu press or wrap the tofu in paper towels and place a weight on top for about 15 minutes.
   - Cut the tofu into bite-sized cubes or rectangles, about 1-inch pieces.
2. **Coat the Tofu:**
   - In a shallow dish, mix the flour and cornstarch.
   - Lightly coat each tofu piece with the flour-cornstarch mixture, shaking off any excess.
3. **Heat the Oil:**
   - Heat vegetable oil in a frying pan over medium heat. You'll need enough oil to cover the bottom of the pan by about 1/2 inch.
   - Once the oil is hot, carefully add the tofu pieces to the pan. Fry in batches if necessary to avoid overcrowding.
4. **Fry the Tofu:**
   - Fry the tofu pieces until they are golden brown and crispy on all sides, about 2-3 minutes per side.
   - Remove the tofu from the pan and drain on paper towels.
5. **Prepare the Dashi Sauce:**
   - In a small saucepan, combine dashi stock, soy sauce, mirin, sake, and sugar (if using).

- Bring to a simmer over medium heat, stirring occasionally. Simmer for a few minutes until the sauce is slightly reduced and flavors are combined.
6. **Assemble and Serve:**
   - Arrange the fried tofu pieces in serving bowls.
   - Spoon the hot dashi sauce over the tofu.
   - Garnish with grated daikon radish, chopped green onions, shredded nori, and grated ginger if desired.
   - Serve immediately.

Tips:

- **Oil Temperature:** Make sure the oil is hot enough before adding the tofu to ensure it gets crispy. If the oil is not hot enough, the tofu may become greasy.
- **Dashi Stock:** You can use homemade dashi or instant dashi powder dissolved in water.
- **Texture:** For an extra crispy texture, double-coat the tofu by dipping it in the flour-cornstarch mixture, then in a light batter, and again in the flour-cornstarch mixture before frying.

Enjoy your Agedashi Tofu with its perfect blend of crispy tofu and savory sauce!

Udon Noodle Salad

Ingredients:

- **12 oz** udon noodles (fresh or frozen)
- **1 cup** shredded carrots
- **1 cup** sliced bell peppers (red, yellow, or orange)
- **1 cup** thinly sliced cucumber
- **1 cup** cherry tomatoes (halved)
- **1/4 cup** sliced green onions
- **1/4 cup** chopped fresh cilantro or parsley (optional)
- **1/4 cup** sesame seeds (toasted, optional)

For the Dressing:

- **1/4 cup** soy sauce
- **2 tablespoons** rice vinegar
- **2 tablespoons** sesame oil
- **1 tablespoon** honey or maple syrup (or to taste)
- **1 teaspoon** grated fresh ginger
- **1 clove** garlic, minced
- **1 teaspoon** sesame seeds (toasted, optional)
- **1 tablespoon** water (to thin out the dressing if needed)

Instructions:

1. **Cook the Udon Noodles:**
   - Bring a large pot of water to a boil. Add the udon noodles and cook according to the package instructions until tender (usually 3-4 minutes for fresh udon or 6-8 minutes for frozen).
   - Drain the noodles and rinse them under cold water to stop the cooking process and cool them down. Toss with a little bit of sesame oil to prevent sticking.
2. **Prepare the Vegetables:**
   - While the noodles are cooking, prepare the vegetables: shred the carrots, slice the bell peppers and cucumber, halve the cherry tomatoes, and chop the green onions and cilantro (if using).
3. **Make the Dressing:**
   - In a small bowl, whisk together soy sauce, rice vinegar, sesame oil, honey or maple syrup, grated ginger, minced garlic, and sesame seeds. Adjust the seasoning to taste. If the dressing is too thick, add a bit of water to reach your desired consistency.
4. **Assemble the Salad:**
   - In a large bowl, combine the cooked udon noodles with the shredded carrots, bell peppers, cucumber, cherry tomatoes, and green onions.
   - Pour the dressing over the salad and toss gently to coat everything evenly.

5. **Serve:**
   - Garnish with chopped cilantro or parsley and toasted sesame seeds if desired.
   - Serve immediately or chill in the refrigerator for about 30 minutes for a colder, more refreshing salad.

Tips:

- **Vegetable Variations:** Feel free to add other vegetables like snap peas, shredded cabbage, or radishes based on your preference.
- **Protein Additions:** For added protein, you can include grilled chicken, tofu, or shrimp.
- **Noodle Alternatives:** If you can't find udon noodles, you can use soba or rice noodles as an alternative.

Enjoy your Udon Noodle Salad as a satisfying and vibrant dish!

Yudofu (Hot Tofu Stew)

Ingredients:

- **1 block (14 oz)** firm tofu (or silken tofu if you prefer a softer texture)
- **4 cups** dashi stock (or vegetable/chicken broth)
- **1 cup** sliced mushrooms (shiitake, enoki, or any variety you like)
- **1 cup** sliced napa cabbage or other leafy greens
- **1-2 green onions**, sliced
- **1-2 carrots**, sliced thinly
- **1 tablespoon** soy sauce (optional, for added flavor)
- **1 tablespoon** mirin (optional, for a touch of sweetness)
- **1 teaspoon** sesame oil (optional, for a richer flavor)

For the Dipping Sauce:

- **2 tablespoons** soy sauce
- **2 tablespoons** mirin
- **1 tablespoon** rice vinegar or lemon juice
- **1 teaspoon** grated ginger
- **1 teaspoon** sesame seeds (toasted, optional)

Garnishes (optional):

- **Chopped green onions**
- **Shredded nori** (seaweed)
- **Toasted sesame seeds**

Instructions:

1. **Prepare the Tofu:**
   - Drain the tofu and press it to remove excess moisture. You can use a tofu press or wrap the tofu in paper towels and place a weight on top for about 15 minutes.
   - Cut the tofu into large cubes.
2. **Prepare the Broth:**
   - In a large pot, heat the dashi stock over medium heat until it begins to simmer. If using store-bought dashi powder, follow the instructions to prepare it.
   - Add soy sauce, mirin, and sesame oil to the broth if you're using them.
3. **Add Vegetables:**
   - Add the sliced mushrooms, napa cabbage, and carrots to the simmering broth. Cook for about 5 minutes, or until the vegetables are tender.
4. **Cook the Tofu:**
   - Gently add the tofu cubes to the pot. Simmer for another 5 minutes, allowing the tofu to warm through and absorb the flavors of the broth.
5. **Prepare the Dipping Sauce:**

- In a small bowl, combine soy sauce, mirin, rice vinegar (or lemon juice), grated ginger, and sesame seeds (if using). Mix well.
6. **Serve:**
   - Ladle the hot tofu stew into individual bowls.
   - Garnish with chopped green onions, shredded nori, and toasted sesame seeds if desired.
   - Serve with the dipping sauce on the side.

Tips:

- **Broth:** For a richer flavor, you can use homemade dashi. Instant dashi powder works well for convenience.
- **Texture:** Silken tofu gives a softer, creamier texture, while firm tofu holds its shape better. Choose based on your preference.
- **Vegetables:** Feel free to customize the vegetables based on what you have on hand. Other options include bok choy, spinach, or snow peas.

Enjoy your warm and soothing Yudofu, perfect for a chilly day or a comforting meal!

Goya Stir-Fry

Ingredients:

- **1 medium bitter melon (goya)**
- **1/2 pound** ground pork (or chicken, beef, or tofu for a vegetarian option)
- **1 medium onion**, sliced
- **1 bell pepper**, sliced (optional, for added color and flavor)
- **2 cloves garlic**, minced
- **1 tablespoon** vegetable oil
- **2 tablespoons** soy sauce
- **1 tablespoon** mirin (or substitute with a teaspoon of sugar and a splash of water)
- **1 tablespoon** sake (or substitute with white wine)
- **1/2 teaspoon** sesame oil
- **Salt and pepper**, to taste
- **1 teaspoon** sesame seeds (toasted, optional)
- **Chopped green onions** (for garnish, optional)

Instructions:

1. **Prepare the Bitter Melon:**
   - Cut the bitter melon in half lengthwise and scoop out the seeds using a spoon.
   - Slice the melon thinly (about 1/4-inch thick).
   - To reduce bitterness, sprinkle the slices with salt and let them sit for 10-15 minutes. Rinse thoroughly under cold water and pat dry with paper towels.
2. **Cook the Ground Meat:**
   - Heat vegetable oil in a large skillet or wok over medium-high heat.
   - Add the ground pork and cook until browned and cooked through, breaking it up into small pieces with a spoon.
3. **Add Vegetables:**
   - Add the sliced onion and bell pepper (if using) to the skillet with the cooked pork. Stir-fry for a few minutes until the vegetables start to soften.
4. **Stir-Fry the Bitter Melon:**
   - Add the sliced bitter melon to the skillet and continue to stir-fry for another 5-7 minutes, until the bitter melon is tender and slightly charred.
5. **Season the Dish:**
   - Add minced garlic and stir well.
   - Stir in soy sauce, mirin, and sake. Cook for another 2-3 minutes until everything is well combined and the sauce slightly reduces.
   - Drizzle with sesame oil and season with salt and pepper to taste.
6. **Serve:**
   - Garnish with toasted sesame seeds and chopped green onions if desired.
   - Serve hot with steamed rice or noodles.

Tips:

- **Bitter Melon:** Adjust the bitterness by altering the amount of salt used during the initial salting process. Rinsing and patting dry helps reduce bitterness.
- **Protein Options:** Ground pork is commonly used, but chicken, beef, or tofu are good alternatives. Adjust cooking times accordingly.
- **Vegetable Variations:** You can add other vegetables such as mushrooms, carrots, or snap peas for more variety.

Enjoy your Goya Stir-Fry, a tasty and nutritious dish with a distinctive flavor!

Shiso and Lemon Rice

Ingredients:

- **2 cups** short-grain or medium-grain rice (Japanese or sushi rice)
- **2 1/2 cups** water (or according to your rice cooker instructions)
- **1 tablespoon** rice vinegar
- **1 tablespoon** sugar
- **1/2 teaspoon** salt
- **1 lemon**, zested and juiced
- **10-12 shiso leaves**, thinly sliced
- **1 tablespoon** sesame seeds (toasted, optional)
- **Chopped green onions** (for garnish, optional)

Instructions:

1. **Prepare the Rice:**
   - Rinse the rice under cold water until the water runs clear. This helps remove excess starch and prevents the rice from becoming too sticky.
   - Cook the rice according to the manufacturer's instructions for your rice cooker or using the stovetop method.
2. **Prepare the Seasoning:**
   - In a small bowl, mix rice vinegar, sugar, and salt until the sugar and salt are dissolved.
3. **Combine and Fluff:**
   - Once the rice is cooked, transfer it to a large bowl and let it cool slightly.
   - While the rice is still warm, drizzle the vinegar mixture over it and gently fold to combine.
   - Add lemon zest and lemon juice to the rice, mixing gently.
4. **Add Shiso Leaves:**
   - Gently fold in the sliced shiso leaves. The heat from the rice will release their aromatic flavor.
5. **Serve:**
   - Garnish with toasted sesame seeds and chopped green onions if desired.
   - Serve warm or at room temperature.

Tips:

- **Shiso Leaves:** Shiso can be found at Asian grocery stores. If you can't find fresh shiso, you can use dried shiso flakes or substitute with mint or basil for a different flavor.
- **Rice Type:** Short-grain or medium-grain rice works best for this recipe, but you can use long-grain rice if needed.
- **Lemon Adjustments:** Adjust the amount of lemon juice and zest according to your taste preferences. You can add more for a stronger lemon flavor or less for a milder one.

Enjoy this refreshing and aromatic Shiso and Lemon Rice as a delightful side dish or light meal!

Cold Soba with Dipping Sauce

Ingredients:

- **8 oz** soba noodles
- **2 cups** water (for boiling noodles)

For the Dipping Sauce:

- **1/2 cup** soy sauce
- **1/4 cup** mirin
- **1/4 cup** dashi stock (or water if you prefer a lighter sauce)
- **1 tablespoon** sugar
- **1 teaspoon** sesame oil (optional, for added flavor)

Optional Toppings:

- **Sliced green onions**
- **Grated daikon radish**
- **Wasabi**
- **Shredded nori** (seaweed)
- **Sesame seeds**
- **Pickled ginger**

Instructions:

1. **Cook the Soba Noodles:**
   - Bring a large pot of water to a boil. Add the soba noodles and cook according to the package instructions (usually 4-6 minutes).
   - Stir occasionally to prevent sticking.
2. **Prepare the Dipping Sauce:**
   - In a saucepan, combine soy sauce, mirin, dashi stock, and sugar.
   - Heat the mixture over medium heat, stirring until the sugar is dissolved and the sauce is well combined. Do not let it boil.
   - Remove from heat and let the sauce cool to room temperature.
3. **Cool the Noodles:**
   - Once the soba noodles are cooked, drain them in a colander.
   - Rinse the noodles under cold running water to cool them down and remove excess starch. Continue rinsing until the water runs clear.
   - Drain the noodles well and transfer them to a serving dish or individual plates.
4. **Serve:**
   - Place the dipping sauce in small bowls for each person.
   - Garnish the cold soba noodles with optional toppings like sliced green onions, grated daikon, shredded nori, sesame seeds, and pickled ginger.
   - Serve immediately.

Tips:

- **Noodle Cooking:** Do not overcook the soba noodles as they can become mushy. Rinse them thoroughly to stop the cooking process.
- **Dipping Sauce:** Adjust the saltiness and sweetness of the dipping sauce according to your taste. You can also add a splash of rice vinegar for a bit of tanginess.
- **Garnishes:** Toppings add extra flavor and texture, so feel free to customize them based on your preference.

Enjoy your Cold Soba with Dipping Sauce as a refreshing and satisfying dish!

Sunomono (Vinegared Salad)

Ingredients:

- **1 medium cucumber** (or 2 small cucumbers)
- **1/2 cup** thinly sliced radishes (optional, for added crunch and color)
- **1/2 cup** cooked and peeled shrimp (optional, for a seafood version)
- **1 tablespoon** sugar
- **1/4 cup** rice vinegar
- **1 tablespoon** soy sauce
- **1/2 teaspoon** salt
- **1/2 teaspoon** sesame oil (optional, for added flavor)

Garnishes (optional):

- **Sesame seeds** (toasted)
- **Chopped green onions**
- **Shredded nori** (seaweed)
- **Pickled ginger**

Instructions:

1. **Prepare the Vegetables:**
   - Wash and peel the cucumber if desired. Slice it thinly using a mandoline or a sharp knife.
   - If using, thinly slice the radishes as well.
2. **Prepare the Shrimp (if using):**
   - If using shrimp, cook and peel them. Slice into smaller pieces if necessary.
3. **Make the Vinegar Dressing:**
   - In a bowl, combine sugar, rice vinegar, soy sauce, salt, and sesame oil (if using). Stir until the sugar and salt are dissolved.
4. **Combine and Marinate:**
   - In a large bowl, combine the sliced cucumber, radishes, and shrimp (if using).
   - Pour the vinegar dressing over the vegetables and shrimp.
   - Toss gently to coat everything evenly.
   - Let the salad marinate for at least 10-15 minutes to allow the flavors to meld. You can also chill it in the refrigerator if you prefer it colder.
5. **Serve:**
   - Garnish with toasted sesame seeds, chopped green onions, shredded nori, or pickled ginger if desired.
   - Serve immediately or keep it chilled until ready to serve.

Tips:

- **Cucumber:** For a crispier texture, you can sprinkle the cucumber slices with salt and let them sit for 10 minutes before rinsing and adding to the salad. This helps to draw out excess moisture.
- **Variations:** Sunomono can be customized with other vegetables like carrots, seaweed (wakame), or even tofu for a different twist.
- **Sweetness:** Adjust the amount of sugar in the dressing to suit your taste. Some people prefer a sweeter or tangier flavor.

Enjoy your Sunomono as a light and refreshing side dish or appetizer!

Japanese Pickles (Tsukemono)

Ingredients:

- **2 small cucumbers** (or 1 large cucumber)
- **1 small eggplant**
- **1 tablespoon** salt
- **1 cup** red shiso leaves (fresh or dried)
- **1/2 cup** rice vinegar
- **1/4 cup** sugar
- **2 tablespoons** soy sauce
- **1 tablespoon** mirin (or a teaspoon of sugar and a splash of water as a substitute)
- **1 teaspoon** sesame seeds (toasted, optional)

Instructions:

1. **Prepare the Vegetables:**
   - Wash the cucumbers and eggplant. Slice the cucumbers into thin rounds or half-moons.
   - Cut the eggplant into thin rounds or small wedges. If using large eggplant, you may want to peel it slightly to reduce bitterness.
2. **Salt the Vegetables:**
   - Place the sliced cucumbers and eggplant in a bowl. Sprinkle with salt and mix well.
   - Let the vegetables sit for about 30 minutes to 1 hour. This will help to draw out moisture and soften them slightly.
3. **Prepare the Pickling Brine:**
   - In a saucepan, combine rice vinegar, sugar, soy sauce, and mirin. Heat over medium heat, stirring until the sugar is completely dissolved. Remove from heat and let cool to room temperature.
   - If using fresh shiso leaves, rinse them and pat dry. If using dried shiso, crumble it into smaller pieces.
4. **Rinse and Drain the Vegetables:**
   - After the vegetables have salted, rinse them under cold water to remove excess salt.
   - Drain them well and pat dry with paper towels.
5. **Combine and Pickle:**
   - In a clean jar or container, layer the cucumbers and eggplant.
   - Pour the cooled pickling brine over the vegetables, making sure they are fully submerged. If necessary, you can use a small plate or weight to keep the vegetables submerged.
6. **Add Shiso:**
   - Add the red shiso leaves to the jar or container, mixing them in with the vegetables.
7. **Refrigerate:**

- Seal the jar or container and refrigerate. Let the pickles marinate for at least 24 hours for the best flavor. They can be stored in the refrigerator for up to a week.

8. **Serve:**
   - Before serving, you can sprinkle toasted sesame seeds over the pickles if desired.

Tips:

- **Shiso Leaves:** If you can't find red shiso, you can use regular shiso or substitute with a bit of dried seaweed for a different flavor.
- **Variations:** You can experiment with other vegetables or add a touch of chili flakes for extra heat.
- **Storage:** Keep the pickles tightly sealed and stored in the refrigerator to maintain their crispness and flavor.

Enjoy your homemade Shibazuke as a refreshing and flavorful addition to your Japanese meals!

Yaki Onigiri (Grilled Rice Balls)

Ingredients:

- **2 cups** cooked Japanese short-grain or sushi rice (preferably cold or at room temperature)
- **1 tablespoon** salt (divided)
- **2 tablespoons** soy sauce
- **1 tablespoon** mirin (or substitute with a teaspoon of sugar and a splash of water)
- **1 teaspoon** vegetable oil (for grilling)
- **Optional fillings:** pickled plums (umeboshi), cooked salmon, or any of your favorite fillings

Instructions:

1. **Prepare the Rice:**
   - Cook the rice according to the package instructions and let it cool slightly. Cold rice is easier to shape.
   - Once cooled, season the rice with 1/2 teaspoon of salt, mixing it evenly.
2. **Shape the Rice Balls:**
   - Wet your hands with water to prevent the rice from sticking.
   - Take a small amount of rice (about 1/4 cup) and form it into a triangle or oval shape. If using a filling, place a small amount in the center of the rice before shaping.
   - Press firmly to ensure the rice ball holds its shape.
3. **Prepare the Glaze:**
   - In a small bowl, mix soy sauce, mirin, and the remaining 1/2 teaspoon of salt. Stir until the salt is dissolved.
4. **Grill the Rice Balls:**
   - Heat a grill pan or non-stick skillet over medium heat. Brush with a little vegetable oil to prevent sticking.
   - Place the rice balls in the pan and grill for about 2-3 minutes on each side, or until they develop a crispy, golden-brown crust.
   - While grilling, brush the rice balls with the soy sauce mixture. Turn and brush the other sides as well.
5. **Serve:**
   - Remove the rice balls from the grill and let them cool slightly.
   - Serve warm or at room temperature.

Tips:

- **Rice Texture:** Using cold rice helps in shaping the balls more easily. Freshly cooked rice tends to be too sticky.

- **Fillings:** Popular fillings include umeboshi (pickled plums), cooked salmon, or even a mixture of chopped pickles. Be sure to keep the filling small to avoid the rice balls falling apart.
- **Glaze Variations:** You can adjust the amount of soy sauce and mirin to suit your taste, or add a splash of sake or honey for a different flavor profile.

Enjoy your Yaki Onigiri as a savory snack or a side dish to complement your meal!

Seaweed Salad

Ingredients:

- **1 cup** dried wakame seaweed
- **1 small cucumber**, thinly sliced
- **1 small carrot**, julienned (optional)
- **2 tablespoons** rice vinegar
- **1 tablespoon** soy sauce
- **1 tablespoon** sesame oil
- **1 tablespoon** sugar
- **1 teaspoon** sesame seeds (toasted)
- **1 tablespoon** chopped fresh cilantro or parsley (optional, for garnish)
- **Chili flakes** (optional, for a bit of heat)

Instructions:

1. **Rehydrate the Seaweed:**
   - Place the dried wakame seaweed in a bowl and cover with warm water. Let it soak for about 10 minutes, or until the seaweed expands and becomes tender.
   - Drain the seaweed and gently squeeze out any excess water. Chop into bite-sized pieces if needed.
2. **Prepare the Vegetables:**
   - Slice the cucumber thinly. If you prefer, you can use a mandoline for consistent thin slices.
   - Julienne the carrot if using.
3. **Make the Dressing:**
   - In a small bowl, whisk together rice vinegar, soy sauce, sesame oil, and sugar until the sugar is dissolved.
4. **Combine Ingredients:**
   - In a large bowl, combine the rehydrated seaweed, cucumber, and carrot.
   - Pour the dressing over the salad and toss to coat everything evenly.
5. **Garnish and Serve:**
   - Sprinkle toasted sesame seeds over the top.
   - Garnish with chopped cilantro or parsley if desired.
   - Add chili flakes for a bit of heat if you like.
6. **Chill (Optional):**
   - For best flavor, let the salad sit in the refrigerator for about 30 minutes before serving. This allows the flavors to meld together.

Tips:

- **Seaweed Variations:** You can also use other types of seaweed like hijiki or kombu, or a seaweed salad mix from the store if preferred.

- **Dressing:** Adjust the amount of sugar and soy sauce according to your taste preferences. You can make it more tangy by adding a bit more vinegar.
- **Texture:** Make sure to rehydrate the seaweed thoroughly to achieve the right texture. Over-soaking can make it too soft, so keep an eye on it.

Enjoy your Seaweed Salad as a refreshing side dish or a light and nutritious appetizer!

Sashimi Salad

Ingredients:

- **6 oz** sashimi-grade fish (such as tuna, salmon, or yellowtail), thinly sliced
- **4 cups** mixed salad greens (such as lettuce, arugula, or spinach)
- **1 small cucumber**, thinly sliced
- **1 small avocado**, sliced
- **1/2 cup** cherry tomatoes, halved
- **1/4 cup** thinly sliced red onion
- **1/4 cup** shredded carrots
- **2 tablespoons** sesame seeds (toasted)
- **2 tablespoons** sliced radishes (optional)

For the Dressing:

- **3 tablespoons** soy sauce
- **2 tablespoons** rice vinegar
- **1 tablespoon** sesame oil
- **1 tablespoon** honey or sugar
- **1 teaspoon** grated ginger
- **1 clove** garlic, minced (optional)
- **1 teaspoon** wasabi paste (optional, for a bit of heat)

Instructions:

1. **Prepare the Vegetables:**
   - Wash and dry the salad greens.
   - Slice the cucumber and avocado, and halve the cherry tomatoes.
   - Thinly slice the red onion and shred the carrots.
2. **Prepare the Dressing:**
   - In a small bowl, whisk together soy sauce, rice vinegar, sesame oil, honey (or sugar), grated ginger, and minced garlic (if using).
   - Add wasabi paste if you like a bit of heat. Adjust the sweetness and acidity to taste.
3. **Assemble the Salad:**
   - Arrange the mixed salad greens on a large serving platter or individual plates.
   - Top with the sliced cucumber, avocado, cherry tomatoes, red onion, shredded carrots, and radishes (if using).
   - Arrange the sashimi slices on top of the salad.
4. **Dress and Garnish:**
   - Drizzle the dressing over the salad just before serving. You can serve the dressing on the side if you prefer.
   - Sprinkle with toasted sesame seeds.
5. **Serve:**

- Serve immediately to enjoy the freshness of the sashimi and the crispness of the vegetables.

Tips:

- **Sashimi Quality:** Ensure that you use sashimi-grade fish from a reputable source to ensure safety and quality.
- **Vegetable Variations:** Feel free to add other vegetables like snap peas, radicchio, or bell peppers based on your preference.
- **Dressing Variations:** You can adjust the dressing ingredients based on your taste, adding more soy sauce for saltiness, more honey for sweetness, or more vinegar for tanginess.

Enjoy your refreshing and elegant Sashimi Salad as a light meal or a beautiful appetizer!

Salmon Teriyaki

Ingredients:

- **4 salmon fillets** (about 6 oz each), skin on or off
- **1 tablespoon** vegetable oil (for cooking)

For the Teriyaki Sauce:

- **1/4 cup** soy sauce
- **1/4 cup** mirin
- **2 tablespoons** sake (or white wine)
- **2 tablespoons** sugar
- **1 clove** garlic, minced (optional)
- **1 teaspoon** grated ginger
- **1 teaspoon** cornstarch mixed with 1 tablespoon water (optional, for thickening)

Garnishes (optional):

- **Sliced green onions**
- **Sesame seeds** (toasted)
- **Chopped cilantro or parsley**

Instructions:

1. **Prepare the Teriyaki Sauce:**
   - In a small saucepan, combine soy sauce, mirin, sake, sugar, garlic (if using), and grated ginger.
   - Bring to a simmer over medium heat, stirring occasionally until the sugar dissolves.
   - If you prefer a thicker sauce, add the cornstarch mixture and stir until the sauce thickens. Remove from heat and let cool slightly.
2. **Prepare the Salmon:**
   - Pat the salmon fillets dry with paper towels and season lightly with salt and pepper.
3. **Cook the Salmon:**
   - **For Pan-Seared Salmon:**
     - Heat vegetable oil in a large skillet over medium-high heat.
     - Add the salmon fillets, skin-side down if the skin is on. Cook for about 4-5 minutes on each side, or until the salmon is cooked through and has a golden-brown crust.
     - In the last minute of cooking, brush the salmon with the teriyaki sauce and allow it to caramelize slightly.
   - **For Grilled Salmon:**
     - Preheat the grill to medium-high heat and brush the grill grates with oil.

- Place the salmon fillets on the grill, skin-side down if the skin is on. Grill for about 4-5 minutes on each side, or until the salmon is cooked through and has grill marks.
- Brush the salmon with the teriyaki sauce during the last minute of grilling.

4. **Serve:**
   - Transfer the cooked salmon to serving plates.
   - Drizzle with additional teriyaki sauce if desired and garnish with sliced green onions, toasted sesame seeds, and chopped cilantro or parsley.

5. **Accompaniments:**
   - Serve with steamed rice and a side of vegetables or a simple salad for a complete meal.

Tips:

- **Salmon Fillets:** If you prefer, you can use salmon steaks or other types of fish, adjusting the cooking time as needed.
- **Sauce Adjustments:** Adjust the sweetness or saltiness of the sauce to your taste by varying the amount of sugar or soy sauce.
- **Marinating:** For extra flavor, you can marinate the salmon in a small amount of teriyaki sauce for 30 minutes before cooking.

Enjoy your homemade Salmon Teriyaki with its rich, savory glaze and perfectly cooked fish!

Miso-Marinated Grilled Eggplant

Ingredients:

- **2 medium eggplants**
- **2 tablespoons** white miso (or red miso for a stronger flavor)
- **1 tablespoon** soy sauce
- **1 tablespoon** mirin (or substitute with a teaspoon of sugar and a splash of water)
- **1 tablespoon** sake (or white wine, optional)
- **1 teaspoon** sesame oil
- **1 tablespoon** sugar (adjust to taste)
- **1 clove** garlic, minced (optional)
- **1 teaspoon** grated ginger (optional)
- **Sesame seeds** (toasted, for garnish)
- **Sliced green onions** (for garnish)

Instructions:

1. **Prepare the Eggplant:**
   - Wash and slice the eggplants into 1/2-inch thick rounds or lengthwise slices.
   - If you like, you can sprinkle the slices with a little salt and let them sit for 15-20 minutes to draw out excess moisture and bitterness. Rinse and pat dry before marinating.
2. **Make the Miso Marinade:**
   - In a small bowl, combine white miso, soy sauce, mirin, sake (if using), sesame oil, and sugar. Mix well until smooth. If using garlic and ginger, add them to the mixture for additional flavor.
3. **Marinate the Eggplant:**
   - Brush the eggplant slices with the miso marinade, making sure they are evenly coated.
   - Allow the eggplant to marinate for at least 15 minutes, or up to 1 hour for a deeper flavor.
4. **Preheat the Grill:**
   - Preheat your grill to medium-high heat. If using a grill pan, preheat it over medium-high heat.
5. **Grill the Eggplant:**
   - Lightly oil the grill grates or grill pan to prevent sticking.
   - Place the eggplant slices on the grill. Cook for about 3-4 minutes on each side, or until they are tender and have nice grill marks. Brush with additional marinade during grilling for extra flavor.
6. **Serve:**
   - Transfer the grilled eggplant to a serving platter.
   - Garnish with toasted sesame seeds and sliced green onions.
7. **Accompaniments:**

- ○ Serve as a side dish with rice, or as an appetizer. It pairs well with other Japanese dishes or can be enjoyed on its own.

Tips:

- **Eggplant Type:** Japanese eggplants are ideal for this recipe due to their tender texture and thinner skin, but regular eggplants work well too.
- **Marinade Variations:** Adjust the sweetness or saltiness of the marinade according to your taste. You can add a splash of rice vinegar for a bit of tanginess.
- **Cooking Method:** If you don't have a grill, you can also cook the eggplant under a broiler or on a stovetop grill pan.

Enjoy your flavorful and savory Miso-Marinated Grilled Eggplant as a delightful addition to your meal!

Cold Chashu Ramen

Ingredients:

For the Chashu:

- **1 lb** pork belly, skin-on
- **1/4 cup** soy sauce
- **1/4 cup** sake (or white wine)
- **1/4 cup** mirin
- **1/4 cup** sugar
- **1 cup** water
- **1 clove** garlic, smashed
- **1 small piece** ginger, sliced
- **1 green onion**, chopped

For the Cold Ramen:

- **2 servings** fresh or dried ramen noodles
- **2 cups** cold chicken or vegetable broth (chilled)
- **1 cucumber**, julienned
- **1/2 cup** shredded carrots
- **1/2 cup** corn kernels (fresh, frozen, or canned)
- **1/4 cup** sliced bamboo shoots (optional)
- **2-3 radishes**, thinly sliced
- **2 soft-boiled eggs** (optional)
- **Nori** (seaweed), cut into strips (optional)
- **Sesame seeds** (toasted)
- **Chopped green onions** (for garnish)
- **Soy sauce** or **sesame oil** (for drizzling)

Instructions:

1. Prepare the Chashu:

- **Sear the Pork Belly:** Heat a large pot or Dutch oven over medium-high heat. Sear the pork belly on all sides until browned.
- **Cook the Chashu:** In the same pot, add soy sauce, sake, mirin, sugar, water, garlic, ginger, and green onion. Bring to a simmer.
- **Simmer:** Cover and reduce heat to low. Simmer for about 1.5 to 2 hours, or until the pork belly is tender. Turn the pork occasionally to ensure even cooking.
- **Cool and Slice:** Once cooked, let the pork belly cool in the liquid. Slice thinly once cooled.

2. Cook the Ramen Noodles:

- **Boil Noodles:** Cook the ramen noodles according to the package instructions. Drain and rinse under cold water to cool them down.
- **Chill:** Place the cooled noodles in the refrigerator until ready to use.

3. Prepare the Toppings:

- **Prepare Vegetables:** Julienne the cucumber, shred the carrots, and slice the radishes.
- **Cook Corn:** If using fresh corn, cook briefly. If using frozen or canned, make sure it's thawed or drained.

4. Assemble the Cold Ramen:

- **Prepare Bowls:** Divide the chilled ramen noodles between serving bowls.
- **Add Toppings:** Arrange the cucumber, carrots, corn, bamboo shoots (if using), and radishes over the noodles.
- **Add Chashu:** Place the slices of chashu pork on top of the noodles.
- **Add Egg (Optional):** Halve the soft-boiled eggs and place them on top of the ramen.

5. Add Broth and Garnish:

- **Add Broth:** Pour the chilled broth over the noodles and toppings.
- **Garnish:** Sprinkle with sesame seeds, chopped green onions, and strips of nori if desired. Drizzle with a bit of soy sauce or sesame oil for extra flavor.

6. Serve:

- Serve immediately and enjoy your refreshing Cold Chashu Ramen!

Tips:

- **Chashu Variations:** You can make chashu in advance and store it in the refrigerator. It can also be enjoyed warm if preferred.
- **Noodle Variations:** If you don't have ramen noodles, other types of Asian noodles such as soba or udon can be used.
- **Broth:** Use a clear, chilled broth to keep the dish light and refreshing. You can make your own or use store-bought.

Enjoy your Cold Chashu Ramen as a delicious and cooling summer meal!

Mentaiko Pasta (Spicy Cod Roe Pasta)

Ingredients:

- **200g (7 oz) spaghetti** (or your preferred pasta)
- **100g (3.5 oz) mentaiko** (spicy cod roe, available at Asian grocery stores)
- **2 tablespoons unsalted butter**
- **2 tablespoons olive oil**
- **2 cloves garlic, minced**
- **1 tablespoon soy sauce**
- **1 tablespoon sake** (optional, can substitute with white wine)
- **1 tablespoon heavy cream** (or more to taste)
- **1 tablespoon chopped green onions** (for garnish)
- **1 tablespoon chopped parsley** (optional, for garnish)
- **Shichimi togarashi** (Japanese seven-spice blend, optional, for extra heat)
- **Salt and black pepper** to taste

Instructions:

1. **Cook the Pasta:**
   - Boil a large pot of salted water and cook the spaghetti according to the package instructions until al dente. Reserve about 1/2 cup of pasta cooking water, then drain the pasta.
2. **Prepare the Mentaiko:**
   - Remove the mentaiko from its membrane and place it in a bowl. If the mentaiko is not pre-seasoned or spicy enough for your taste, you can mix in a bit of shichimi togarashi or chili flakes to enhance the spiciness.
3. **Make the Sauce:**
   - In a large skillet or pan, heat the olive oil and butter over medium heat. Add the minced garlic and cook until fragrant, but not browned, about 1 minute.
   - Add the mentaiko to the pan and cook for another 1-2 minutes, stirring well to combine with the garlic.
4. **Combine Ingredients:**
   - Pour in the soy sauce and sake (or white wine), and cook for an additional minute to reduce slightly.
   - Stir in the heavy cream and cook for another 1-2 minutes until the sauce is well combined and creamy. You can adjust the amount of cream based on how creamy you want the sauce to be.
5. **Mix Pasta and Sauce:**
   - Add the cooked spaghetti to the pan with the sauce. Toss well to ensure the pasta is evenly coated with the sauce. If the sauce is too thick, add a little of the reserved pasta cooking water to loosen it up.
6. **Finish and Serve:**

- Season with salt and black pepper to taste. Garnish with chopped green onions and parsley, if using.
- Serve immediately, optionally with a sprinkle of additional shichimi togarashi for extra heat.

Enjoy your homemade Mentaiko Pasta!

Japanese Corn Tempura

Ingredients:

- **2 ears of fresh corn**
- **1 cup all-purpose flour**
- **1/2 cup cornstarch**
- **1/2 teaspoon baking powder**
- **1 cup cold sparkling water** (or very cold water)
- **1/2 teaspoon salt**
- **Vegetable oil** (for frying)
- **Sea salt** (for seasoning, optional)
- **Lemon wedges** (for serving, optional)

Instructions:

1. **Prepare the Corn:**
   - Husk the corn and remove all the silk. Cut the corn kernels off the cobs. You can use a knife to carefully slice the kernels off or a corn stripper if you have one.
2. **Prepare the Tempura Batter:**
   - In a large bowl, whisk together the flour, cornstarch, baking powder, and salt.
   - Gradually add the cold sparkling water, gently stirring until just combined. The batter should be lumpy; don't overmix, as it can result in a less crispy texture.
3. **Heat the Oil:**
   - In a large, deep skillet or pot, heat about 2 inches of vegetable oil over medium-high heat. You can test the oil temperature by dropping a small amount of batter into it; it should rise to the surface and start bubbling.
4. **Coat and Fry the Corn:**
   - Dip the corn kernels into the tempura batter, allowing any excess to drip off.
   - Carefully drop the battered corn kernels into the hot oil. Fry in small batches to avoid overcrowding. Fry for about 2-3 minutes, or until the tempura is golden and crispy.
   - Use a slotted spoon to remove the tempura from the oil and drain on a plate lined with paper towels.
5. **Season and Serve:**
   - Season the tempura with a pinch of sea salt, if desired, while still warm.
   - Serve immediately with lemon wedges on the side for a fresh, zesty contrast.

Enjoy your crispy, sweet Corn Tempura as a tasty appetizer or snack!

Zaru Udon (Cold Udon Noodles)

Ingredients:

For the Noodles:

- **300g (10 oz) udon noodles** (fresh or frozen; dried udon can also be used, but follow package instructions for cooking)
- **Ice water** (for chilling)

For the Dipping Sauce (Tsuyu):

- **1 cup dashi stock** (you can use instant dashi powder mixed with water if you don't have homemade dashi)
- **1/4 cup soy sauce**
- **1/4 cup mirin** (sweet rice wine)
- **1 tablespoon sugar** (optional, to taste)

For Garnish (optional but recommended):

- **2-3 green onions**, finely sliced
- **1 tablespoon grated daikon radish**
- **Nori seaweed**, cut into thin strips
- **Sesame seeds**
- **Wasabi** (for a spicy kick, if desired)

Instructions:

1. **Prepare the Noodles:**
   - If using fresh or frozen udon noodles, follow the package instructions to cook them. Generally, you'll boil them for 2-4 minutes.
   - Once cooked, drain the noodles and immediately transfer them to a bowl of ice water to cool and stop the cooking process. This also helps to firm up the texture.
   - After cooling, drain the noodles again and set aside.
2. **Make the Dipping Sauce:**
   - In a saucepan, combine the dashi stock, soy sauce, mirin, and sugar (if using). Heat over medium heat and stir until the sugar dissolves. You do not need to boil the mixture.
   - Let the dipping sauce cool to room temperature. You can refrigerate it if you prefer it chilled.
3. **Assemble and Serve:**
   - Arrange the chilled udon noodles on a serving plate or bamboo mat (zaru) for an authentic presentation.
   - Serve the dipping sauce in small individual bowls or cups.

- Garnish with your choice of green onions, grated daikon, nori strips, sesame seeds, and wasabi.

4. **How to Eat:**
   - To eat, take a portion of udon noodles, dip them into the dipping sauce, and enjoy. You can mix the garnishes into the dipping sauce or sprinkle them directly onto the noodles if you prefer.

Zaru Udon is versatile and allows for customization based on your taste and available ingredients. Enjoy your refreshing and satisfying dish!

Ikayaki (Grilled Whole Squid)

Ingredients:

- **4 whole squid** (cleaned and gutted, with heads and tentacles removed)
- **2 tablespoons soy sauce**
- **2 tablespoons mirin** (sweet rice wine)
- **2 tablespoons sake** (Japanese rice wine) or dry white wine
- **1 tablespoon sugar**
- **1 clove garlic, minced** (optional)
- **1 teaspoon grated ginger** (optional)
- **Lemon wedges** (for serving)
- **Chopped green onions** (for garnish, optional)
- **Shichimi togarashi** (Japanese seven-spice blend, optional, for extra flavor)

Instructions:

1. **Prepare the Squid:**
   - Clean the squid thoroughly if not already done. Remove the beak from the center of the tentacles and the cartilage from the body.
   - Pat the squid dry with paper towels.
2. **Make the Sauce:**
   - In a small bowl, combine soy sauce, mirin, sake, sugar, garlic, and ginger (if using). Stir until the sugar is dissolved and the mixture is well combined.
3. **Marinate the Squid:**
   - Brush the squid with a portion of the sauce, making sure to coat both the inside and outside. Let it marinate for about 15-30 minutes.
4. **Grill the Squid:**
   - Preheat your grill or a grill pan over medium-high heat. If using a grill pan, lightly oil it to prevent sticking.
   - Grill the squid for about 2-3 minutes per side, or until they are cooked through and have a nice char. Brush with additional sauce during grilling for extra flavor.
   - Be careful not to overcook the squid, as it can become rubbery.
5. **Serve:**
   - Once grilled, transfer the squid to a serving plate.
   - Cut the squid into manageable pieces or leave it whole, depending on your preference.
   - Serve with lemon wedges and garnish with chopped green onions and shichimi togarashi if desired.

Tips:

- **Grilling Temperature:** Make sure your grill or pan is hot enough to create a good sear but not so hot that it burns the squid before it cooks through.

- **Marination:** If you have time, marinating the squid longer will enhance the flavor. Just be careful not to over-marinate as the soy sauce can make the squid too salty.

Enjoy your homemade Ikayaki with a side of rice or as an appetizer!

Sweet Corn Soup

Ingredients:

- **4 cups fresh or frozen corn kernels** (about 4-5 ears of corn if using fresh)
- **1 medium onion**, finely chopped
- **2 cloves garlic**, minced
- **2 tablespoons butter** (or olive oil for a lighter option)
- **4 cups vegetable or chicken broth**
- **1 cup milk** (or heavy cream for a richer soup)
- **1-2 tablespoons all-purpose flour** (optional, for thickening)
- **Salt and black pepper** to taste
- **1 teaspoon sugar** (optional, to enhance sweetness)
- **Chopped fresh parsley or chives** (for garnish)
- **Croutons or a drizzle of cream** (optional, for serving)

Instructions:

1. **Prepare the Corn:**
   - If using fresh corn, remove the husks and silk, then cut the kernels off the cobs. Set aside.
2. **Cook the Aromatics:**
   - In a large pot, melt the butter over medium heat. Add the chopped onion and cook until translucent, about 5 minutes.
   - Add the minced garlic and cook for an additional 1-2 minutes, until fragrant.
3. **Add the Corn:**
   - Stir in the corn kernels and cook for another 5 minutes, allowing them to soften slightly.
4. **Make the Soup Base:**
   - Add the broth to the pot and bring to a simmer. Cook for 10-15 minutes, until the corn is tender.
5. **Blend the Soup:**
   - Using an immersion blender, blend the soup until smooth. If you don't have an immersion blender, you can carefully transfer the soup in batches to a regular blender. Be cautious as the soup will be hot.
6. **Add Milk/Cream:**
   - Return the blended soup to the pot (if using a regular blender). Stir in the milk or heavy cream and heat through. If the soup is too thick, you can add a bit more broth or milk to reach your desired consistency.
7. **Thicken the Soup (Optional):**
   - If you prefer a thicker soup, mix the flour with a small amount of cold milk or water to make a slurry, then stir it into the soup. Cook for a few more minutes until thickened.
8. **Season:**

- Taste the soup and season with salt, black pepper, and sugar if desired.
9. **Serve:**
   - Ladle the soup into bowls. Garnish with chopped parsley or chives and add croutons or a drizzle of cream if desired.

Enjoy your Sweet Corn Soup as a warm and comforting meal!

Tuna Tataki

Ingredients:

For the Tuna:

- **200-300g (7-10 oz) fresh tuna steak** (sushi-grade)
- **Salt and black pepper**, to taste
- **1-2 tablespoons vegetable oil** (for searing)
- **1 tablespoon sesame seeds** (optional, for coating)

For the Marinade/Dipping Sauce:

- **3 tablespoons soy sauce**
- **2 tablespoons rice vinegar**
- **1 tablespoon mirin** (sweet rice wine)
- **1 teaspoon sugar** (optional, for a touch of sweetness)
- **1 teaspoon grated ginger**
- **1 clove garlic, minced**
- **1 teaspoon sesame oil**
- **1 tablespoon chopped green onions** (for garnish)
- **1 tablespoon toasted sesame seeds** (optional, for garnish)

Optional Garnishes:

- **Thinly sliced radishes**
- **Thinly sliced cucumber**
- **Wasabi**
- **Pickled ginger**

Instructions:

1. **Prepare the Tuna:**
   - Pat the tuna steak dry with paper towels. Season both sides with salt and black pepper.
   - If you're using sesame seeds, press the seeds into the surface of the tuna steak for a bit of texture and flavor.
2. **Sear the Tuna:**
   - Heat the vegetable oil in a skillet over high heat. Once the oil is hot, add the tuna steak.
   - Sear the tuna for about 30 seconds to 1 minute on each side, depending on your desired level of doneness. The outside should be browned, while the inside remains rare to medium-rare.
   - Remove the tuna from the skillet and let it rest for a few minutes before slicing.
3. **Make the Marinade/Dipping Sauce:**

- In a small bowl, whisk together soy sauce, rice vinegar, mirin, sugar (if using), grated ginger, minced garlic, and sesame oil.

4. **Slice the Tuna:**
   - Slice the seared tuna into thin slices, about 1/4 inch thick. Arrange the slices on a serving plate.

5. **Serve:**
   - Drizzle or serve the marinade/dipping sauce on the side.
   - Garnish with chopped green onions and toasted sesame seeds.
   - Optionally, serve with thinly sliced radishes, cucumber, wasabi, and pickled ginger.

Tips:

- **Searing Temperature:** Make sure the skillet is very hot before adding the tuna to get a good sear without overcooking the inside.
- **Slicing:** For best results, use a sharp knife and slice the tuna against the grain.

Enjoy your Tuna Tataki as a delicious, light, and elegant dish!

Japanese Style Potato Salad

Ingredients:

- **4 medium potatoes** (Russet or Yukon Gold are good choices)
- **1/2 cup Japanese mayonnaise** (Kewpie is a popular brand, but any good-quality mayo will work)
- **1 tablespoon rice vinegar** (or white vinegar)
- **1 teaspoon Dijon mustard** (optional, for a bit of tang)
- **1/2 teaspoon sugar**
- **1/2 teaspoon salt**, or to taste
- **1/4 teaspoon black pepper**, or to taste
- **1 small carrot**, peeled and diced
- **1/2 cucumber**, thinly sliced or diced
- **1/4 cup finely chopped onion** (optional, for added flavor)
- **1/4 cup cooked ham**, diced (optional)
- **Chopped parsley or chives** (for garnish, optional)

Instructions:

1. **Prepare the Potatoes:**
   - Peel and cut the potatoes into evenly sized chunks.
   - Place the potatoes in a pot of cold, salted water and bring to a boil. Cook until the potatoes are tender and can be easily pierced with a fork, about 10-15 minutes.
   - Drain the potatoes and let them cool slightly.
2. **Prepare the Vegetables:**
   - While the potatoes are cooking, peel and dice the carrot. You can either boil the carrot in the same pot as the potatoes for about 5 minutes until tender, or sauté it lightly.
   - If using cucumber, slice it thinly and lightly salt it to draw out excess moisture. Pat dry with a paper towel before adding it to the salad.
   - If using onion, finely chop and rinse under cold water to reduce its sharpness. Drain well.
3. **Make the Dressing:**
   - In a small bowl, mix together the Japanese mayonnaise, rice vinegar, Dijon mustard (if using), sugar, salt, and black pepper. Adjust seasoning to taste.
4. **Assemble the Salad:**
   - Once the potatoes are cool enough to handle, cut them into bite-sized pieces and transfer them to a large bowl.
   - Gently mash the potatoes with a fork or potato masher, leaving some chunks for texture.
   - Add the diced carrot, cucumber, onion (if using), and ham (if using) to the bowl.
   - Pour the dressing over the potato mixture and gently fold it in until all ingredients are well coated.

5. **Chill and Serve:**
   - Cover the salad and refrigerate for at least 30 minutes to allow the flavors to meld.
   - Before serving, garnish with chopped parsley or chives if desired.

Tips:

- **Texture:** Some people prefer a smoother texture, while others like a chunkier potato salad. Adjust the mashing to your preference.
- **Add-ins:** You can also include other vegetables like peas or corn, or adjust the recipe to suit your taste.

Enjoy your Japanese-style potato salad as a delicious and creamy side dish!

Shrimp and Avocado Salad

Ingredients:

- **450g (1 lb) large shrimp**, peeled and deveined
- **2 tablespoons olive oil**
- **1 clove garlic**, minced
- **Salt and black pepper**, to taste
- **1 teaspoon paprika** (optional, for extra flavor)
- **1 tablespoon lemon juice** (or lime juice)
- **2 ripe avocados**, diced
- **1 small cucumber**, diced
- **1/4 red onion**, thinly sliced
- **1 small bell pepper**, diced (any color)
- **2 cups mixed greens** (such as arugula, spinach, or romaine)
- **2 tablespoons fresh cilantro or parsley**, chopped (optional, for garnish)

For the Dressing:

- **3 tablespoons olive oil**
- **2 tablespoons lemon juice** (or lime juice)
- **1 teaspoon Dijon mustard**
- **1 teaspoon honey** (optional, for a touch of sweetness)
- **1 clove garlic**, minced
- **Salt and black pepper**, to taste

Instructions:

1. **Prepare the Shrimp:**
   - In a large bowl, toss the shrimp with olive oil, minced garlic, salt, black pepper, and paprika (if using).
   - Heat a skillet over medium-high heat. Add the shrimp and cook for 2-3 minutes per side, or until they are opaque and cooked through. The shrimp should be pink and firm. Remove from heat and let them cool slightly.
   - Drizzle with lemon juice.
2. **Make the Dressing:**
   - In a small bowl or jar, whisk together olive oil, lemon juice, Dijon mustard, honey (if using), minced garlic, salt, and black pepper until well combined.
3. **Assemble the Salad:**
   - In a large salad bowl, combine the mixed greens, diced avocados, cucumber, red onion, and bell pepper.
   - Add the cooked shrimp to the salad.
4. **Dress the Salad:**
   - Drizzle the dressing over the salad and toss gently to combine all the ingredients. Be careful not to mash the avocado.

5. **Garnish and Serve:**
   - Garnish with chopped cilantro or parsley if desired.
   - Serve immediately for the freshest taste.

Tips:

- **Shrimp Preparation:** Ensure shrimp are not overcooked, as they can become tough. They cook quickly, so keep an eye on them.
- **Avocado:** If preparing the salad in advance, you might want to wait to add the avocado until just before serving to prevent it from browning.

Enjoy your Shrimp and Avocado Salad as a refreshing, protein-packed meal!

Nasu Dengaku (Miso Glazed Eggplant)

Ingredients:

- **2 medium eggplants**
- **2 tablespoons vegetable oil** (for brushing)
- **1/4 cup red miso paste** (or white miso for a milder flavor)
- **2 tablespoons mirin** (sweet rice wine)
- **2 tablespoons sake** (Japanese rice wine) or dry white wine
- **2 tablespoons sugar**
- **1 tablespoon soy sauce**
- **1 teaspoon sesame oil**
- **1 teaspoon grated ginger** (optional, for added flavor)
- **1 tablespoon chopped green onions** (for garnish, optional)
- **Sesame seeds** (for garnish, optional)

Instructions:

1. **Prepare the Eggplants:**
   - Cut the eggplants in half lengthwise. If they're large, you may want to cut them into quarters or smaller pieces to ensure even cooking.
   - Use a knife to score the flesh of the eggplant in a crosshatch pattern, being careful not to cut through the skin. This will help the glaze penetrate and ensure even cooking.
2. **Preheat the Oven or Grill:**
   - If using a broiler, preheat it to high.
   - If using a grill, preheat it to medium-high heat.
3. **Make the Miso Glaze:**
   - In a small saucepan, combine the miso paste, mirin, sake, sugar, soy sauce, sesame oil, and grated ginger (if using).
   - Heat over medium heat, stirring frequently, until the mixture is smooth and slightly thickened. This should take about 3-5 minutes. Remove from heat and let it cool slightly.
4. **Cook the Eggplants:**
   - Brush the cut sides of the eggplant with vegetable oil.
   - Place the eggplants cut-side down on a baking sheet if using a broiler or on the grill. Cook until the cut sides are golden brown and the eggplant is tender, about 5-7 minutes under the broiler or 10-15 minutes on the grill. You may need to turn them occasionally to ensure even cooking.
5. **Apply the Miso Glaze:**
   - Once the eggplants are cooked, turn them cut-side up.
   - Brush or spoon the miso glaze over the eggplant halves, spreading it evenly.
6. **Broil or Grill the Glazed Eggplant:**

- If using a broiler, return the eggplants to the broiler and cook for an additional 2-3 minutes, or until the glaze is bubbly and slightly caramelized. Keep an eye on them to prevent burning.
- If using a grill, you can also brush the glaze on and close the grill lid, allowing it to caramelize slightly.

7. **Garnish and Serve:**
   - Transfer the eggplants to a serving plate.
   - Garnish with chopped green onions and sesame seeds if desired.

Tips:

- **Eggplant Texture:** If you find that eggplant soaks up too much oil or becomes too greasy, you can sprinkle a bit of salt on the cut sides before cooking to draw out excess moisture. Rinse and pat dry before cooking.
- **Miso Glaze:** Adjust the sweetness or saltiness of the glaze by adding more sugar or soy sauce to taste.

Enjoy your Nasu Dengaku as a delicious side dish or appetizer!

Tonkotsu Ramen (Pork Bone Broth Ramen)

Ingredients:

For the Pork Broth:

- **3-4 pounds (1.5-2 kg) pork bones** (preferably a mix of neck bones, leg bones, and/or trotters)
- **1 onion**, peeled and quartered
- **2-3 cloves garlic**, smashed
- **1-inch piece of ginger**, sliced
- **2-3 green onions**, chopped
- **Water**, as needed (for boiling)

For the Tonkotsu Ramen:

- **4-6 ounces ramen noodles** (fresh or dried)
- **1 tablespoon vegetable oil** (for sautéing)
- **1-2 cups sliced pork belly** or pork shoulder (optional, for additional toppings)
- **1-2 eggs** (soft-boiled or marinated)
- **1 cup sliced mushrooms** (shiitake or other types)
- **1 cup bean sprouts** (optional)
- **1-2 cups spinach** (or bok choy)
- **1-2 tablespoons soy sauce** (for seasoning the broth)
- **1-2 tablespoons miso paste** (optional, for added depth of flavor)

For Garnish:

- **Chopped green onions**
- **Nori seaweed**, cut into strips
- **Sesame seeds**
- **Pickled ginger** (optional)
- **Shichimi togarashi** (Japanese seven-spice blend, optional)

Instructions:

1. Prepare the Pork Broth:

1. **Blanch the Bones:**
   - Place the pork bones in a large pot and cover with cold water. Bring to a boil over high heat.
   - Boil for about 5 minutes, then drain and discard the water. Rinse the bones under cold water to remove any scum or impurities.
2. **Cook the Broth:**
   - Return the cleaned bones to the pot and cover with fresh water.

- Add the onion, garlic, ginger, and green onions.
- Bring to a boil, then reduce the heat to a simmer.
- Simmer for 4-6 hours, occasionally skimming off any foam or fat that rises to the surface. For a richer broth, you can simmer up to 12 hours. Add more water as necessary to keep the bones covered.

3. **Strain the Broth:**
   - Once the broth has developed a rich, milky texture and deep flavor, strain it through a fine-mesh sieve into another pot. Discard the solids.

2. Prepare the Toppings and Noodles:

1. **Cook the Pork Belly (Optional):**
   - In a skillet, heat vegetable oil over medium-high heat. Add the pork belly slices and cook until they are crispy and browned on both sides. Set aside.
2. **Prepare the Ramen Noodles:**
   - Cook the ramen noodles according to package instructions. Drain and set aside.
3. **Prepare Additional Toppings:**
   - Lightly sauté the mushrooms in a separate pan until tender.
   - Blanch the spinach or bok choy in boiling water for 1-2 minutes, then drain and set aside.

3. Assemble the Ramen:

1. **Season the Broth:**
   - Heat the strained broth and season it with soy sauce and miso paste (if using). Adjust seasoning to taste.
2. **Assemble the Bowls:**
   - Divide the cooked noodles among serving bowls.
   - Ladle the hot broth over the noodles.
   - Arrange the pork belly, mushrooms, bean sprouts, spinach, and any other toppings on top of the noodles.
3. **Add Garnishes:**
   - Top each bowl with chopped green onions, nori strips, sesame seeds, pickled ginger, and shichimi togarashi if desired.
4. **Add the Egg:**
   - Halve the soft-boiled or marinated egg and place it on top of the ramen.

Tips:

- **Broth Clarity:** For a clearer broth, skim off the fat and impurities more frequently during simmering.
- **Marinated Egg:** To make a marinated egg, soak soft-boiled eggs in a mixture of soy sauce, mirin, and a little sugar for a few hours before serving.

Enjoy your homemade Tonkotsu Ramen with its rich and satisfying flavor!

Agedashi Eggplant

Ingredients:

For the Eggplant:

- **2 medium eggplants**
- **1/4 cup all-purpose flour** (for dusting)
- **1/4 cup cornstarch** (for coating)
- **Vegetable oil** (for frying)

For the Sauce:

- **1 cup dashi stock** (you can use instant dashi powder mixed with water if you don't have homemade dashi)
- **2 tablespoons soy sauce**
- **2 tablespoons mirin** (sweet rice wine)
- **1 tablespoon sake** (Japanese rice wine) or dry white wine
- **1 tablespoon sugar** (optional, for a touch of sweetness)
- **1 teaspoon grated ginger** (optional, for extra flavor)

For Garnish:

- **Chopped green onions**
- **Grated daikon radish** (optional)
- **Shredded nori seaweed**
- **Shichimi togarashi** (Japanese seven-spice blend, optional)
- **Sesame seeds** (optional)

Instructions:

1. **Prepare the Eggplant:**
   - Cut the eggplants into bite-sized cubes or slices, depending on your preference. If the eggplant is large, you might want to cut it into smaller pieces to ensure even cooking.
   - Place the cut eggplant in a bowl of salted water for about 15 minutes to remove excess bitterness. This step is optional but can help with the texture and flavor.
   - Drain the eggplant and pat it dry thoroughly with paper towels.
2. **Prepare for Frying:**
   - In a shallow bowl, mix together the flour and cornstarch.
   - Lightly coat each piece of eggplant with the flour-cornstarch mixture, shaking off any excess.
3. **Fry the Eggplant:**

- Heat about 2 inches of vegetable oil in a deep skillet or frying pan over medium-high heat. Test the oil temperature by dropping in a small piece of bread; it should sizzle and brown within 30 seconds.
- Fry the eggplant pieces in batches, being careful not to overcrowd the pan. Fry until golden brown and crispy, about 3-4 minutes per batch.
- Use a slotted spoon to transfer the fried eggplant to a plate lined with paper towels to drain excess oil.

4. **Make the Sauce:**
   - In a saucepan, combine the dashi stock, soy sauce, mirin, sake, and sugar (if using). Heat over medium heat, stirring occasionally, until the sugar dissolves and the sauce is warmed. Add the grated ginger if using.

5. **Assemble the Dish:**
   - Arrange the fried eggplant pieces on a serving plate or bowl.
   - Pour the warm sauce over the eggplant or serve the sauce on the side for dipping.
   - Garnish with chopped green onions, grated daikon radish, shredded nori seaweed, shichimi togarashi, and sesame seeds if desired.

Tips:

- **Oil Temperature:** Make sure the oil is at the right temperature to ensure crispy eggplant. If the oil is too cool, the eggplant will absorb too much oil and become soggy.
- **Serving:** Agedashi Eggplant is best served immediately after frying while it's still crispy. If preparing in advance, you can reheat the eggplant in a hot oven to crisp it up before serving.

Enjoy your homemade Agedashi Eggplant with its delightful contrast of crispy texture and savory flavor!

Umeboshi (Pickled Plum) Rice Balls

Ingredients:

For the Rice Balls:

- **2 cups short-grain or sushi rice**
- **2 1/2 cups water**
- **1/2 teaspoon salt**
- **4-6 umeboshi plums** (pitted and chopped, or use umeboshi paste)
- **1 tablespoon sesame seeds** (optional, for coating)
- **Nori seaweed**, cut into strips (optional, for wrapping)

For Seasoning the Rice:

- **1-2 tablespoons rice vinegar**
- **1 tablespoon sugar** (optional, for a touch of sweetness)
- **1/2 teaspoon salt**

Instructions:

1. **Cook the Rice:**
   - Rinse the rice under cold water until the water runs clear to remove excess starch. Drain well.
   - In a rice cooker or pot, combine the rinsed rice and water. Cook according to the rice cooker instructions or bring to a boil, then cover and simmer on low heat for 15-20 minutes until the water is absorbed and the rice is tender.
   - Remove from heat and let it sit covered for 10 minutes to allow the rice to steam and firm up.
2. **Season the Rice:**
   - While the rice is still warm, transfer it to a large bowl.
   - In a small bowl, mix the rice vinegar, sugar (if using), and salt until dissolved.
   - Gently fold the vinegar mixture into the warm rice with a wooden spatula or spoon. Let the rice cool to a manageable temperature for handling.
3. **Prepare the Umeboshi:**
   - If using whole umeboshi plums, remove the pits and finely chop the flesh. If using umeboshi paste, it's ready to use as is.
4. **Form the Rice Balls:**
   - Wet your hands with water to prevent the rice from sticking. Take a small handful of rice (about 2-3 tablespoons) and flatten it slightly in your palm.
   - Place a small amount of umeboshi or umeboshi paste in the center of the rice.
   - Gently mold the rice around the filling, shaping it into a triangle or ball. Press gently to ensure it holds together but avoid compressing too hard, as it can make the rice too dense.
5. **Optional Coating:**

- If desired, roll the rice balls in sesame seeds or wrap them with a strip of nori seaweed for added flavor and texture.

6. **Serve:**
   - Umeboshi rice balls can be enjoyed immediately or stored in an airtight container at room temperature for a few hours. If storing for longer, keep them in the refrigerator and allow them to come to room temperature before eating.

Tips:

- **Handling Rice:** Wetting your hands helps prevent the rice from sticking and makes it easier to form the rice balls.
- **Rice Consistency:** The rice should be slightly sticky but not too wet. If it's too dry, it may be hard to mold.

Enjoy your Umeboshi Rice Balls as a flavorful and convenient snack or part of a meal!

Japanese Summer Rolls

Ingredients:

For the Summer Rolls:

- **8-10 rice paper wrappers** (medium or large size)
- **1 cup cooked shrimp**, peeled and deveined (or use tofu for a vegetarian option)
- **1 cup cooked vermicelli noodles** (optional)
- **1 cup julienned carrots**
- **1 cup julienned cucumber**
- **1 cup shredded lettuce** (or baby spinach)
- **1/2 cup fresh cilantro leaves**
- **1/2 cup fresh mint leaves**
- **1/2 cup fresh basil leaves** (optional, for additional flavor)

For the Dipping Sauce:

- **1/4 cup soy sauce**
- **1 tablespoon rice vinegar**
- **1 tablespoon honey** or sugar
- **1 teaspoon sesame oil**
- **1 teaspoon grated ginger**
- **1 clove garlic**, minced
- **1 tablespoon chopped peanuts** (optional, for garnish)
- **1-2 teaspoons Sriracha** (optional, for a spicy kick)

Instructions:

1. Prepare the Ingredients:

- **Cook and Prepare Shrimp:** If using shrimp, cook them in boiling water for 2-3 minutes until pink and opaque. Drain and let cool, then slice in half lengthwise if they are large.
- **Prepare Noodles:** If using vermicelli noodles, cook according to package instructions, then rinse under cold water and drain.
- **Prepare Vegetables:** Julienne the carrots and cucumber. Shred the lettuce or spinach.

2. Make the Dipping Sauce:

- In a small bowl, whisk together the soy sauce, rice vinegar, honey (or sugar), sesame oil, grated ginger, minced garlic, and Sriracha (if using).
- Taste and adjust seasoning if needed. Garnish with chopped peanuts if desired.

3. Assemble the Summer Rolls:

1. **Soak Rice Paper Wrappers:**

- Fill a large bowl with warm water. Dip one rice paper wrapper into the water for about 10-15 seconds, or until it becomes pliable but still slightly firm. Carefully remove it from the water and lay it flat on a clean surface or a damp kitchen towel.

2. **Add Fillings:**
   - Arrange a small amount of lettuce, carrots, cucumber, cilantro, mint, and basil (if using) in the center of the rice paper, leaving about 2 inches on each side.
   - Place a few shrimp halves or tofu slices on top of the vegetables. If using vermicelli noodles, add a small amount as well.

3. **Roll the Summer Rolls:**
   - Fold the sides of the rice paper over the filling, then roll it up from the bottom, tucking in the sides as you go. The rice paper will stick together, sealing the roll.

4. **Repeat:**
   - Repeat the process with the remaining rice paper wrappers and fillings.

4. Serve:

- Arrange the summer rolls on a serving platter and serve with the dipping sauce on the side.

Tips:

- **Rice Paper Handling:** Be gentle with the rice paper as it can tear easily. If it becomes too soft, it may be difficult to handle, so work quickly.
- **Variations:** You can customize the fillings based on your preferences or what you have on hand. Other popular additions include sliced bell peppers, avocado, or cooked chicken.

Enjoy your Japanese Summer Rolls as a fresh and flavorful meal or snack!

Cold Tofu with Soy Sauce and Green Onions

Ingredients:

- **1 block of firm or silken tofu** (about 300g or 10 oz)
- **2-3 tablespoons soy sauce**
- **1-2 teaspoons sesame oil**
- **1-2 green onions**, finely sliced
- **1 teaspoon grated ginger** (optional)
- **1 teaspoon toasted sesame seeds** (optional, for garnish)
- **Shredded nori seaweed** (optional, for garnish)

Instructions:

1. **Prepare the Tofu:**
   - **Drain and Slice:** If using a block of tofu, drain it well. For firm tofu, you can cut it into bite-sized cubes or slices. For silken tofu, simply cut it into smaller pieces or leave it whole if preferred.
   - **Chill:** For best results, chill the tofu in the refrigerator for at least 30 minutes before serving.
2. **Prepare the Dressing:**
   - **Combine Ingredients:** In a small bowl, mix the soy sauce with the sesame oil. If using, you can add the grated ginger to the dressing for extra flavor.
3. **Assemble the Dish:**
   - **Place Tofu:** Arrange the tofu on a serving plate or individual dishes.
   - **Add Dressing:** Drizzle the soy sauce and sesame oil mixture over the tofu.
4. **Garnish:**
   - **Add Toppings:** Sprinkle the finely sliced green onions on top of the tofu. Garnish with toasted sesame seeds and shredded nori seaweed if desired.
5. **Serve:**
   - Serve the cold tofu immediately as a side dish or appetizer. It pairs well with steamed rice and other Japanese dishes.

Tips:

- **Tofu Texture:** Silken tofu has a delicate texture and is more suited for eating cold, while firm tofu has a denser texture that holds up well in various dishes.
- **Chilling:** Chilling the tofu enhances its texture and flavor. If you're short on time, you can serve it at room temperature, but it's best when cold.
- **Flavor Variations:** You can experiment with additional toppings such as finely chopped fresh herbs, a dash of rice vinegar, or a sprinkle of shichimi togarashi for added spice.

Enjoy your Cold Tofu with Soy Sauce and Green Onions as a light and tasty addition to any meal!

Okra with Soy Sauce and Sesame

Ingredients:

- **1/2 pound (225g) fresh okra** (about 15-20 pods)
- **1 tablespoon vegetable oil** (or sesame oil)
- **1-2 tablespoons soy sauce**
- **1 teaspoon sesame oil**
- **1 tablespoon toasted sesame seeds**
- **1-2 cloves garlic**, minced (optional, for extra flavor)
- **1 teaspoon finely grated ginger** (optional, for added depth)
- **Chopped green onions** (for garnish, optional)
- **Red pepper flakes** (optional, for a bit of heat)

Instructions:

1. **Prepare the Okra:**
   - **Wash and Trim:** Rinse the okra under cold water. Pat dry with paper towels. Trim off the stems and any tough ends.
   - **Cut the Okra:** Slice the okra into 1/4 to 1/2-inch pieces. You can also leave them whole if you prefer.
2. **Cook the Okra:**
   - **Heat Oil:** In a skillet or pan, heat the vegetable oil over medium-high heat. If using sesame oil, you can substitute half of the vegetable oil with sesame oil for extra flavor.
   - **Sauté Garlic and Ginger (Optional):** If using, add the minced garlic and grated ginger to the pan. Sauté for about 30 seconds until fragrant.
   - **Add Okra:** Add the sliced okra to the pan. Stir-fry for about 5-7 minutes, or until the okra is tender but still crisp. Avoid overcooking, as okra can become slimy if cooked too long.
3. **Season the Okra:**
   - **Add Soy Sauce and Sesame Oil:** Drizzle the soy sauce and sesame oil over the cooked okra. Toss to coat evenly.
   - **Add Sesame Seeds:** Sprinkle the toasted sesame seeds over the okra and toss to combine.
4. **Garnish and Serve:**
   - **Garnish:** If desired, garnish with chopped green onions and a sprinkle of red pepper flakes for a touch of heat.
   - **Serve:** Serve the okra warm or at room temperature. It pairs well with rice or as a side dish for various Asian meals.

Tips:

- **Freshness:** Use fresh okra for the best texture and flavor. Avoid using okra that is too large or old, as it can be tough and have a more pronounced slime.
- **Toasted Sesame Seeds:** Lightly toast sesame seeds in a dry pan over medium heat until they become golden and fragrant. This enhances their flavor.
- **Avoid Overcooking:** To keep the okra from becoming slimy, cook it quickly over high heat.

Enjoy your Okra with Soy Sauce and Sesame as a tasty and healthy side dish!

Grilled Mackerel

Ingredients:

- **2 whole mackerel** (about 300-400g each), cleaned and gutted
- **1-2 tablespoons sea salt** (or kosher salt)
- **1-2 tablespoons vegetable oil** (for greasing the grill)
- **Lemon wedges** (for serving, optional)
- **Shredded daikon radish** (for serving, optional)
- **Chopped green onions** (for garnish, optional)

Instructions:

1. Prepare the Mackerel:

- **Clean the Fish:** Rinse the mackerel under cold water and pat dry with paper towels. Make sure the fish is well-cleaned and any remaining innards are removed.
- **Season:** Rub the sea salt evenly over the mackerel, inside and out. Let the salted fish sit for about 15-30 minutes. This process helps to firm up the fish and enhances its flavor.

2. Preheat the Grill:

- **Grill Preparation:** Preheat your grill to medium-high heat. If using a charcoal grill, allow the coals to burn down until they are covered with a light layer of ash. If using a gas grill, preheat with the lid closed.
- **Oil the Grill Grates:** Lightly oil the grill grates with a paper towel dipped in vegetable oil to prevent sticking.

3. Grill the Mackerel:

- **Grilling:** Place the mackerel on the grill. Grill for about 4-6 minutes per side, depending on the thickness of the fish. The fish should be cooked through and have nice grill marks. The skin should be crispy and the flesh opaque.
- **Turn Carefully:** Use a spatula or tongs to turn the mackerel carefully to avoid breaking it apart.

4. Serve:

- **Serving:** Transfer the grilled mackerel to a serving plate.
- **Garnish:** Serve with lemon wedges and shredded daikon radish on the side. You can also sprinkle chopped green onions for added freshness.
- **Accompaniments:** Grilled mackerel goes well with steamed rice and a simple vegetable side, such as sautéed greens or pickled vegetables.

Tips:

- **Freshness:** Use the freshest mackerel available for the best flavor. Look for fish with firm flesh and clear eyes.
- **Avoid Overcooking:** Mackerel cooks quickly and can become dry if overcooked. Keep an eye on it and adjust grilling times based on the thickness of the fillets.
- **Alternative Cooking Methods:** If you don't have a grill, you can also cook mackerel under a broiler or in a hot skillet on the stovetop.

Enjoy your grilled mackerel with its rich, savory flavors and crispy skin!

Chicken Karaage (Japanese Fried Chicken)

Ingredients:

For the Marinade:

- **1 lb (450g) boneless, skinless chicken thighs** (cut into bite-sized pieces)
- **1 tablespoon soy sauce**
- **1 tablespoon sake** (Japanese rice wine) or dry white wine
- **1 tablespoon mirin** (sweet rice wine)
- **1 tablespoon grated ginger**
- **2 cloves garlic**, minced

For the Coating:

- **1 cup all-purpose flour**
- **1/2 cup cornstarch**
- **1/2 teaspoon baking powder**
- **1/2 teaspoon salt**
- **1/2 teaspoon black pepper**
- **1/2 teaspoon paprika** (optional, for color and flavor)
- **Vegetable oil** (for deep-frying)

For Garnish:

- **Lemon wedges**
- **Chopped parsley or shiso leaves** (optional)
- **Shredded cabbage** (optional, for serving)

Instructions:

1. Marinate the Chicken:

- **Combine Ingredients:** In a bowl, mix together the soy sauce, sake, mirin, grated ginger, and minced garlic.
- **Marinate:** Add the chicken pieces to the marinade. Mix well to ensure all pieces are coated. Cover and refrigerate for at least 30 minutes, or up to 2 hours for more intense flavor.

2. Prepare the Coating:

- **Mix Dry Ingredients:** In a large bowl or shallow dish, combine the flour, cornstarch, baking powder, salt, black pepper, and paprika.
- **Coat Chicken:** Remove the marinated chicken from the refrigerator. Dredge each piece in the flour mixture, ensuring an even coating. Shake off any excess flour.

3. Heat the Oil:

- **Heat Oil:** In a large pot or deep skillet, heat about 2 inches of vegetable oil to 350°F (175°C). Use a thermometer to check the temperature. If you don't have a thermometer, test the oil by dropping in a small piece of bread; it should sizzle and brown in about 30 seconds.

4. Fry the Chicken:

- **Fry in Batches:** Carefully add the coated chicken pieces to the hot oil, being careful not to overcrowd the pot. Fry in batches if necessary. Cook for about 4-6 minutes per batch, or until the chicken is golden brown and cooked through (internal temperature should reach 165°F or 74°C).
- **Drain:** Use a slotted spoon or tongs to remove the chicken from the oil and transfer to a plate lined with paper towels to drain excess oil.

5. Serve:

- **Garnish:** Serve the chicken hot, garnished with lemon wedges and chopped parsley or shiso leaves if desired.
- **Optional:** Accompany with shredded cabbage for a traditional touch.

Tips:

- **Marinating Time:** Don't skip the marinating step; it infuses the chicken with flavor and helps keep it juicy.
- **Crispy Coating:** The cornstarch in the coating mixture helps create a light and crispy texture. For extra crispiness, you can double-coat the chicken by dipping it in the flour mixture a second time before frying.
- **Oil Temperature:** Maintaining the correct oil temperature is crucial for achieving a crispy exterior. If the oil is too hot, the coating may burn before the chicken is cooked through. If it's too cool, the coating will become greasy.

Enjoy your homemade Chicken Karaage with its crunchy, flavorful coating and juicy chicken inside!

Spicy Tuna Sushi Rolls

Ingredients:

For the Spicy Tuna:

- **1/2 pound (225g) sushi-grade tuna** (finely chopped)
- **2 tablespoons mayonnaise** (preferably Japanese Kewpie mayo for a richer flavor)
- **1 tablespoon sriracha** (adjust to taste for spiciness)
- **1 teaspoon soy sauce**
- **1 teaspoon sesame oil** (optional)
- **1 teaspoon chopped green onions** (optional)

For the Sushi Rolls:

- **2 cups sushi rice** (uncooked)
- **2 1/2 cups water**
- **1/2 cup rice vinegar**
- **1/4 cup sugar**
- **1 teaspoon salt**
- **10 sheets nori (seaweed)**
- **1 cucumber**, julienned (for added crunch, optional)
- **1 avocado**, sliced (optional)

For Serving:

- **Soy sauce**
- **Pickled ginger**
- **Wasabi**

Instructions:

1. Prepare the Sushi Rice:

- **Cook the Rice:** Rinse the sushi rice under cold water until the water runs clear. Combine the rice and water in a rice cooker or pot. Cook according to the rice cooker instructions or bring to a boil, then cover and simmer on low heat for 15-20 minutes. Remove from heat and let it sit covered for 10 minutes.
- **Season the Rice:** In a small bowl, mix the rice vinegar, sugar, and salt until dissolved. Gently fold the mixture into the cooked rice while it's still warm. Let the rice cool to room temperature.

2. Prepare the Spicy Tuna:

- **Mix Ingredients:** In a bowl, combine the chopped tuna with mayonnaise, sriracha, soy sauce, and sesame oil (if using). Mix until well combined. Add chopped green onions if desired.

3. Assemble the Sushi Rolls:

- **Prepare Nori:** Place a sheet of nori on a bamboo sushi mat lined with plastic wrap, shiny side down.
- **Spread the Rice:** Wet your hands to prevent sticking, then take about 1/2 to 3/4 cup of sushi rice and spread it evenly over the nori, leaving about 1 inch of nori at the top edge free of rice.
- **Add Fillings:** In a line along the bottom edge of the rice, place a small amount of spicy tuna, cucumber, and avocado slices (if using).
- **Roll the Sushi:** Using the bamboo mat, carefully lift the edge of the nori closest to you and start rolling it over the filling, pressing gently but firmly to keep the roll tight. Roll until you reach the exposed edge of nori. Seal the roll by pressing the edge of the nori against the roll.

4. Cut the Sushi Rolls:

- **Slice:** Using a sharp knife coated with a little water or rice vinegar to prevent sticking, cut the roll into 6-8 pieces. Clean the knife between cuts to keep the slices neat.

5. Serve:

- **Arrange:** Place the sushi rolls on a serving platter. Serve with soy sauce, pickled ginger, and wasabi on the side.

Tips:

- **Rice Handling:** Wetting your hands when handling the sushi rice prevents it from sticking. You can also use a little rice vinegar on your hands.
- **Tight Rolling:** Use the bamboo mat to help you roll tightly, but be gentle to avoid squeezing the ingredients out.
- **Chopping Tuna:** Ensure you use sushi-grade tuna for safety and freshness. Chop it finely for the best texture in the spicy tuna mixture.

Enjoy your homemade Spicy Tuna Sushi Rolls with their perfect balance of creamy, spicy, and savory flavors!

Teriyaki Chicken Salad

Ingredients:

For the Teriyaki Chicken:

- **2 boneless, skinless chicken breasts**
- **1/4 cup teriyaki sauce** (store-bought or homemade)
- **1 tablespoon vegetable oil** (for cooking)

For the Salad:

- **4 cups mixed salad greens** (such as lettuce, spinach, and arugula)
- **1 cup shredded carrots**
- **1 cup cucumber**, sliced or julienned
- **1/2 cup cherry tomatoes**, halved
- **1/4 cup red onion**, thinly sliced (optional)
- **1/4 cup sliced radishes** (optional)
- **1/4 cup chopped cilantro** (optional)

For the Teriyaki Dressing:

- **1/4 cup teriyaki sauce** (store-bought or homemade)
- **2 tablespoons rice vinegar**
- **1 tablespoon sesame oil**
- **1 teaspoon honey** or sugar
- **1 teaspoon grated ginger** (optional)
- **1 clove garlic**, minced (optional)

For Garnish:

- **Toasted sesame seeds**
- **Chopped green onions**
- **Crushed crispy wonton strips** or **chow mein noodles** (optional, for crunch)

Instructions:

1. Prepare the Teriyaki Chicken:

- **Marinate:** Place the chicken breasts in a shallow dish and pour 1/4 cup of teriyaki sauce over them. Let marinate for at least 30 minutes, or up to 2 hours in the refrigerator.
- **Cook the Chicken:** Heat the vegetable oil in a skillet over medium-high heat. Remove the chicken from the marinade and cook for about 6-8 minutes per side, or until fully cooked and the internal temperature reaches 165°F (74°C). Alternatively, you can grill the chicken over medium heat for about 6-8 minutes per side.

- **Rest and Slice:** Once cooked, let the chicken rest for a few minutes, then slice into thin strips.

2. Prepare the Salad:

- **Assemble Salad:** In a large salad bowl, combine the mixed salad greens, shredded carrots, cucumber, cherry tomatoes, red onion, radishes, and cilantro.

3. Make the Teriyaki Dressing:

- **Combine Ingredients:** In a small bowl, whisk together the teriyaki sauce, rice vinegar, sesame oil, honey (or sugar), grated ginger, and minced garlic until well combined. Adjust the seasoning to taste if needed.

4. Assemble the Salad:

- **Add Chicken:** Top the salad with the sliced teriyaki chicken.
- **Dress the Salad:** Drizzle the teriyaki dressing over the salad. Toss gently to combine, or serve the dressing on the side for individual servings.

5. Garnish and Serve:

- **Garnish:** Sprinkle toasted sesame seeds, chopped green onions, and crispy wonton strips or chow mein noodles over the salad for added texture and flavor.
- **Serve:** Serve immediately while the chicken is still warm and the salad is fresh.

Tips:

- **Customizations:** Feel free to add other vegetables or toppings to the salad, such as avocado, bell peppers, or snap peas.
- **Homemade Teriyaki Sauce:** If you prefer homemade teriyaki sauce, combine 1/4 cup soy sauce, 2 tablespoons mirin, 2 tablespoons honey or sugar, 1 tablespoon rice vinegar, and 1 teaspoon cornstarch (mixed with a bit of water) in a saucepan. Simmer until slightly thickened.
- **Chicken Variations:** You can also use chicken thighs or even rotisserie chicken for convenience.

Enjoy your Teriyaki Chicken Salad with its delicious combination of savory chicken, crisp vegetables, and a tangy dressing!

Japanese Fruit Parfait

Ingredients:

For the Parfait:

- **1 cup plain Greek yogurt** (or custard, if preferred)
- **2 tablespoons honey** or maple syrup (for sweetness, adjust to taste)
- **1 cup granola** (store-bought or homemade)
- **1-2 cups fresh fruits** (such as strawberries, blueberries, kiwi, mango, or bananas)
- **Mint leaves** (for garnish, optional)
- **Chopped nuts** (such as almonds or walnuts, optional)

For the Fruit Compote (Optional):

- **1 cup mixed berries** (fresh or frozen)
- **2 tablespoons sugar** (or to taste)
- **1 tablespoon lemon juice**
- **1/2 teaspoon vanilla extract** (optional)

Instructions:

1. Prepare the Fruit Compote (Optional):

- **Cook the Compote:** In a small saucepan, combine the mixed berries, sugar, lemon juice, and vanilla extract (if using). Cook over medium heat, stirring occasionally, until the fruit breaks down and the mixture thickens, about 5-10 minutes. Allow it to cool before using.

2. Prepare the Fruits:

- **Wash and Slice:** Wash the fresh fruits thoroughly. Slice or chop them into bite-sized pieces. Arrange them in a bowl or on a plate.

3. Assemble the Parfait:

- **Layering:** In a serving glass or bowl, start by adding a layer of yogurt or custard at the bottom.
- **Add Granola:** Follow with a layer of granola.
- **Add Fruits:** Layer on the fresh fruits or fruit compote if using. You can mix and match fruits or layer them in various patterns.
- **Repeat Layers:** Repeat the layers until the glass is full, ending with a layer of fruit on top.

4. Garnish and Serve:

- **Garnish:** Drizzle honey or maple syrup over the top layer. Garnish with fresh mint leaves and chopped nuts if desired.
- **Serve:** Serve immediately to enjoy the contrasting textures of creamy yogurt, crunchy granola, and fresh fruit.

Tips:

- **Seasonal Fruits:** Use seasonal fruits for the best flavor and freshness. You can also use canned or frozen fruits if fresh ones are not available.
- **Custard Option:** For a richer dessert, you can use vanilla custard instead of yogurt. Simply prepare or buy custard and use it in place of yogurt.
- **Granola:** Choose your favorite granola or make your own by mixing oats with honey or maple syrup and baking until crisp.

Enjoy your Japanese Fruit Parfait as a refreshing and delicious dessert that's perfect for any occasion!

Soba Noodle Soup

Ingredients:

For the Broth:

- **4 cups dashi stock** (Japanese soup stock, you can use instant dashi granules or make it from scratch)
- **1/4 cup soy sauce**
- **2 tablespoons mirin** (sweet rice wine)
- **1 tablespoon sake** (Japanese rice wine) or dry white wine
- **1 tablespoon sugar** (optional, adjust to taste)

For the Soup:

- **200g (7 oz) soba noodles** (fresh or dried)
- **1-2 green onions**, thinly sliced
- **1/2 cup mushrooms**, such as shiitake or button, sliced
- **1 cup baby spinach** or other leafy greens
- **1/2 cup shredded carrots** (optional)
- **1/2 cup tofu cubes** (optional, for added protein)
- **1 sheet nori** (seaweed), cut into strips (optional)

For Garnish:

- **Sesame seeds**
- **Chopped fresh cilantro or green onions**
- **Shredded daikon radish** (optional)
- **Pickled ginger** (optional)

Instructions:

1. Prepare the Broth:

- **Combine Ingredients:** In a large pot, combine the dashi stock, soy sauce, mirin, sake, and sugar (if using). Bring to a simmer over medium heat. Adjust the seasoning to taste, if needed.

2. Cook the Soba Noodles:

- **Boil Noodles:** Cook the soba noodles according to the package instructions. Usually, this involves boiling them in a separate pot of water for 4-5 minutes. Fresh soba noodles might cook faster than dried ones.
- **Drain and Rinse:** Once cooked, drain the noodles and rinse them under cold water to stop the cooking process and remove excess starch. Set aside.

3. Prepare Soup Ingredients:

- **Cook Vegetables:** If using mushrooms, sauté them in a separate pan until tender. If using tofu, you can lightly pan-fry or cube it as desired.
- **Add to Broth:** Add the cooked mushrooms, tofu, and any other vegetables to the simmering broth. Cook for a few minutes until the vegetables are tender.

4. Assemble the Soup:

- **Combine Noodles and Broth:** Divide the cooked soba noodles among serving bowls. Ladle the hot broth and vegetables over the noodles.
- **Add Greens:** Top with baby spinach or other leafy greens, which will wilt slightly from the heat of the broth.

5. Garnish and Serve:

- **Add Garnishes:** Garnish with sesame seeds, chopped green onions, shredded daikon radish, pickled ginger, and nori strips as desired.
- **Serve:** Serve hot and enjoy!

Tips:

- **Dashi Stock:** Dashi is a key component of the broth and provides a deep umami flavor. You can use instant dashi granules for convenience or make it from scratch using kombu (sea kelp) and bonito flakes (dried fish flakes).
- **Customize Toppings:** Feel free to customize the soup with your favorite vegetables, proteins, or additional garnishes.
- **Noodle Texture:** Be careful not to overcook the soba noodles, as they can become mushy if left in the broth for too long. It's best to add them to the bowls just before serving.

Enjoy your homemade Soba Noodle Soup as a warm and nourishing meal!

Yakisoba (Fried Noodles)

Ingredients:

For the Yakisoba:

- **200g (7 oz) yakisoba noodles** (fresh or pre-cooked; if using dried, cook according to package instructions)
- **1 tablespoon vegetable oil** (or sesame oil)
- **1/2 onion**, thinly sliced
- **1 carrot**, julienned or thinly sliced
- **1 cup cabbage**, shredded
- **1 cup mushrooms**, sliced (shiitake, button, or any preferred type)
- **1/2 bell pepper**, thinly sliced (optional)
- **2 cloves garlic**, minced
- **1 tablespoon ginger**, grated (optional)

For the Sauce:

- **1/4 cup soy sauce**
- **2 tablespoons Worcestershire sauce**
- **2 tablespoons ketchup**
- **1 tablespoon oyster sauce** (optional, for extra umami)
- **1 tablespoon sugar** or honey
- **1 tablespoon mirin** (optional, for a touch of sweetness)

For Garnish:

- **Pickled ginger** (beni shoga)
- **Aonori** (dried seaweed flakes) or **shredded nori**
- **Katsuobushi** (dried bonito flakes, optional)
- **Chopped green onions**

Instructions:

1. Prepare the Noodles:

- **Cook the Noodles:** If using dried yakisoba noodles, cook them according to the package instructions. Fresh or pre-cooked yakisoba noodles can be used directly. Drain and set aside.

2. Make the Sauce:

- **Combine Ingredients:** In a small bowl, mix together the soy sauce, Worcestershire sauce, ketchup, oyster sauce (if using), sugar or honey, and mirin (if using). Stir until well combined and the sugar is dissolved.

3. Stir-Fry the Vegetables:

- **Heat Oil:** In a large skillet or wok, heat the vegetable oil over medium-high heat.
- **Cook Aromatics:** Add the garlic and ginger (if using) and cook for about 30 seconds until fragrant.
- **Add Vegetables:** Add the onion, carrot, cabbage, mushrooms, and bell pepper (if using). Stir-fry for about 4-5 minutes until the vegetables are tender-crisp.

4. Add the Noodles and Sauce:

- **Add Noodles:** Add the cooked yakisoba noodles to the skillet or wok.
- **Add Sauce:** Pour the sauce over the noodles and vegetables. Stir well to combine and ensure the noodles are evenly coated with the sauce. Continue to cook for another 2-3 minutes until everything is heated through.

5. Serve:

- **Garnish:** Transfer the yakisoba to serving plates or bowls. Garnish with pickled ginger, aonori, katsuobushi (if using), and chopped green onions.

Tips:

- **Protein Options:** You can add cooked chicken, pork, beef, shrimp, or tofu to the dish. Simply cook the protein first, then add it to the noodles along with the vegetables.
- **Vegetable Variations:** Feel free to customize the vegetables based on what you have on hand. Broccoli, snap peas, or bean sprouts are good alternatives.
- **Noodle Texture:** If the noodles are sticking together, you can add a splash of water or additional sauce to help separate them and keep them moist.

Enjoy your homemade Yakisoba as a delicious and satisfying meal that captures the essence of Japanese comfort food!

Miso-Glazed Zucchini

Ingredients:

- **2 medium zucchinis**, sliced into 1/4-inch rounds or half-moons
- **2 tablespoons white miso paste** (or red miso for a deeper flavor)
- **1 tablespoon soy sauce**
- **1 tablespoon mirin** (sweet rice wine) or honey
- **1 tablespoon rice vinegar** or lemon juice
- **1 tablespoon vegetable oil** (for cooking)
- **1 teaspoon sesame oil** (optional, for extra flavor)
- **1 tablespoon sesame seeds** (for garnish)
- **Chopped green onions** (for garnish, optional)

Instructions:

1. Prepare the Miso Glaze:

- **Combine Ingredients:** In a small bowl, mix together the white miso paste, soy sauce, mirin (or honey), and rice vinegar (or lemon juice) until smooth. Adjust the seasoning to taste if needed. The glaze should be slightly sweet and tangy with a rich umami flavor.

2. Cook the Zucchini:

- **Heat Oil:** In a large skillet or pan, heat the vegetable oil over medium-high heat.
- **Cook Zucchini:** Add the zucchini slices to the skillet in a single layer. Cook for about 2-3 minutes on each side, or until they are golden brown and tender. If you have a lot of zucchini, cook them in batches to avoid overcrowding the pan.

3. Glaze the Zucchini:

- **Add Glaze:** Reduce the heat to medium-low. Pour the miso glaze over the zucchini slices in the pan. Stir gently to coat the zucchini evenly with the glaze.
- **Caramelize:** Continue to cook for an additional 2-3 minutes, or until the glaze has thickened slightly and caramelized around the zucchini. Be careful not to burn the glaze.

4. Finish and Serve:

- **Add Sesame Oil:** If using, drizzle the sesame oil over the zucchini for added flavor.
- **Garnish:** Transfer the miso-glazed zucchini to a serving dish. Sprinkle with sesame seeds and chopped green onions if desired.
- **Serve:** Serve warm as a side dish or over rice for a complete meal.

Tips:

- **Miso Paste:** You can use different types of miso paste based on your flavor preference. White miso is milder and sweeter, while red miso is stronger and saltier.
- **Adjust Sweetness:** If you prefer a sweeter glaze, adjust the amount of mirin or honey. For a more savory glaze, use less sugar or honey.
- **Additional Veggies:** Feel free to add other vegetables like bell peppers or carrots if desired. Just make sure they are cut to similar sizes for even cooking.

Enjoy your Miso-Glazed Zucchini as a tasty and nutritious addition to your meal!

Summer Vegetable Tempura

Ingredients:

For the Tempura:

- **1 medium zucchini**, sliced into rounds or half-moons
- **1 small eggplant**, sliced into rounds or sticks
- **1 red bell pepper**, sliced into strips
- **1 cup baby carrots**, or regular carrots sliced into thin sticks
- **1 cup mushrooms**, such as shiitake or button, cleaned and sliced if large
- **1 cup sweet potatoes**, peeled and sliced into thin rounds (optional)

For the Tempura Batter:

- **1 cup all-purpose flour**
- **1/2 cup cornstarch**
- **1 teaspoon baking powder**
- **1/2 teaspoon salt**
- **1 cup ice-cold sparkling water** (or cold water)
- **1 large egg** (optional, for extra crispiness)

For Frying:

- **Vegetable oil** (such as canola or sunflower oil)

For the Dipping Sauce (Tentsuyu):

- **1/2 cup dashi stock** (you can use instant dashi granules or make it from scratch)
- **1/4 cup soy sauce**
- **2 tablespoons mirin** (sweet rice wine)
- **1 tablespoon sugar** (optional, adjust to taste)

For Garnish:

- **Shredded daikon radish** (optional)
- **Chopped green onions** (optional)
- **Grated ginger** (optional)

Instructions:

1. Prepare the Vegetables:

- **Slice Vegetables:** Wash and cut the vegetables into appropriate sizes. Ensure that the pieces are uniform in size to ensure even cooking.

2. Make the Tempura Batter:

- **Mix Dry Ingredients:** In a bowl, combine the flour, cornstarch, baking powder, and salt.
- **Add Wet Ingredients:** In a separate bowl, lightly beat the egg (if using) and then add it to the dry ingredients. Slowly mix in the ice-cold sparkling water (or cold water) until just combined. The batter should be lumpy; do not overmix.

3. Prepare the Dipping Sauce (Tentsuyu):

- **Combine Ingredients:** In a small saucepan, combine the dashi stock, soy sauce, mirin, and sugar (if using). Heat over medium heat until the sugar dissolves and the sauce is well combined. Allow it to cool before serving.

4. Heat the Oil:

- **Prepare Oil:** In a deep pot or frying pan, heat about 2 inches of vegetable oil to 350°F (175°C). Use a thermometer to check the temperature. If you don't have a thermometer, test the oil by dropping a small piece of batter into it; it should float and sizzle.

5. Fry the Vegetables:

- **Coat and Fry:** Dip each vegetable piece into the tempura batter, allowing excess batter to drip off. Carefully place the battered vegetables into the hot oil. Fry in batches to avoid overcrowding. Cook for about 2-4 minutes per batch, or until golden brown and crispy.
- **Drain:** Use a slotted spoon to remove the tempura from the oil and drain on a plate lined with paper towels.

6. Serve:

- **Arrange:** Arrange the tempura on a serving plate. Garnish with shredded daikon radish, chopped green onions, and grated ginger if desired.
- **Accompany:** Serve with the dipping sauce (tentsuyu) on the side.

Tips:

- **Cold Batter:** Keeping the batter cold is key to achieving a light and crispy texture. The ice-cold sparkling water helps make the batter crispy.
- **Oil Temperature:** Maintain a consistent oil temperature to ensure the tempura cooks evenly and stays crispy. If the oil temperature drops too low, the tempura may become greasy.
- **Vegetable Variations:** Feel free to experiment with other vegetables like snap peas, bell peppers, or green beans.

Enjoy your homemade Summer Vegetable Tempura with its delightful crunch and delicious flavor!

Milton Keynes UK
Ingram Content Group UK Ltd.
UKHW050253300824
447552UK00011B/76

9 798330 360697